The Prostitute in the Pulpit

The Curse of Adam

Mark Elliot Copeland

Copyright © 2002 by Mark Elliot Copeland C.S.W.

The Prostitute in the Pulpit
by Mark Elliot Copeland C.S.W.

Printed in the United States of America

Library of Congress Control Number: 2002112305
ISBN 1-591602-02-5

All rights reserved. No part of this publication may be reproduced or transmitted in any form or by any means without written permission of the publisher.

Xulon Press
11350 Random Hills Road
Suite 800
Fairfax, VA 22030
(703) 279-6511
XulonPress.com

To order additional copies,
call 1-866-909-BOOK (2665).

Contents

Chapter 1
Come Out From Among Her! 11

Chapter 2
Do You Sweat? 19

Chapter 3
The Auction Block 33

Chapter 4
Oh, America! 39

Chapter 5
The Betrayal! 47

Chapter 6
The Story of an Infidel 53

Chapter 7
The Evil Eye! 61

Chapter 8
The Tyrant 67

Chapter 9
　The Unbreakable 75

Chapter 10
　No Weapon Formed Against Us Shall Prosper.....85

Chapter 11
　Yesterday 91

Introduction: Home?

This book is a testimonial of my life and experience as a minister and a social service administrator for the past fifteen years. During these years, I have looked in amazement at the plight of the traditional nuclear family and its genealogical makeup. Many statistics have indicated that majority of children in the United States live with single parents or in second-marriage families. These statistics are not surprising or alarming to me, for this is what I see on a daily basis. One of my many roles as a social service provider is to be familiar with the community I serve.

I have had the good fortune to be able to work in many cities throughout the country, which has afforded me the opportunity to observe communities, churches, and families. What I have witnessed over these years is nothing less than genocide. I have seen crack houses, abandoned houses, dilapidated houses, and welfare houses, but I rarely saw a home. I rarely saw a home were the children were free to grow up in the nurture and love of their mother. To the contrary, I regularly observed children of all ages roaming the streets unsupervised and unprotected, looking for love and affection in all the wrong places. I rarely saw a home where the father was present and a positive role model for his children and a loving husband to his wife. I rarely saw a home that depended on the work ethic of the father, instead of the generosity of the state, to feed his children.

I began to ask myself these following questions. Why are there so many families that are dysfunctional, unstructured, and spiritually devoid of true Christian character and biblical ethics? Why are so many children roaming the streets of America? Why is juvenile crime running rampant? Why are children coming home from school to parentless houses? Why are so many youth today turned out on sex and strung out on drugs? I realize that this depiction is true not only in cities where I have worked and ministered, but is self-evident throughout the world.

This book will attempt to show the results of people who have turned away from the Holy Scriptures and cleaved to the doctrines of demons. One of many purposes of this book is to expose the curse of Adam, which many women unknowingly or knowingly embrace. When a woman works outside of her home

Introduction: Home?

under the authority of someone other than her husband, she is spiritually and physically placing herself under the authority of someone else. The Bible is consistent about the roles of husbands and wives. In writing this book, I am also indicting myself, for I had willingly, yet unknowingly, supported my wife in working outside of the home where she took on the role of provider. However, the Bible clearly states that this responsibility is the husband's.

My support for my wifes working was based on a lack of knowledge of God's Word. I was brought up in the modern-day corporate church, and raised by loving and supportive parents who loved and cared for me dearly. The Bible says, *"Study to show thyself approved unto God, a workman that needeth not to be ashamed, rightly dividing the word of truth" (2 Tim. 2:15)*. Therefore, I enrolled in a Bible college. I studied eschatology, theology, apologetics, and a variety of other subjects that the modern-day preacher is told he should be knowledgeable in to be accepted in the pulpits of America. I sang in the choir and supported the teachings of my pastor. I sacrificed my time and talents to be a good member of my local church. However, I realized that my commitment was not based on sound biblical teaching. *"And Samuel said, Hath the Lord as great delight in burnt offerings and sacrifices, as in obeying the voice of the Lord? Behold, to obey is better than sacrifice, and to hearken than the fat of rams" (1 Sam. 15:22)*.

God says, *"My people are destroyed for lack of*

knowledge: because thou hast rejected knowledge, I will also reject thee, that thou shalt be no priest to me: seeing thou hast forgotten the law of thy God, I will also forget thy children" (Hos. 4:6). In today's modern-day church, men are encouraged to seek out Christian women who have careers or at least career prospects. Many men have been trained to seek out women who can cook, labor in the work force, clean the house, look pretty, and still perform her motherly duties to her children while fulfilling her commitment to her husband. I will refer to these as virtually impossible women. One of many purposes for writing this book is to unveil the perversion that has taken place within the so-called "Christian" home and the modern-day church. Jesus says, "Why call me Lord, Lord, when you do not do what I say?" My hope is that this book, even though it may appear to be strong medicine for some, would be an eye-opening realization for others. For we have certainly witnessed a generation without a home!

Chapter One:

Come Out From Among Her!

*I*n this day of great moral decay and the absence of genuine parental guidance, the church should be a beacon of light that shines hope to a dying society. The revolution of the great harlot has infiltrated the world and has decimated the biblical beliefs of many. The harlot revolution is depicted in the Bible as a false church acting as if it were the true church of Jesus Christ. This adulterous church has blasphemed God's Word and has led many astray. During this generation we have seen hypocrisy in the upper echelon of our modern-day churches and from those who stand behind the pulpit and claim to be messengers of God.

In Revelation, chapters 17 through 19 (please read!), you will find that the Apostle John forewarned us of this day. He told us of a worldwide religious movement that would entice the whole world. I call this time the great harlot revolution! The Apostle John called this religious movement the Great Mother of Harlots (Rev. 17:5). If you are called a mother, it implies that you have children. When we attend church, we become the offspring of what we are taught in the church. The modern-day corporate church is the whore who perverts its members by teaching a damnable doctrine. My friends, take time to observe what is happening around you. Look and see how this generation conducts itself. Many young ladies lose their virginity in their early teenage years. Our society is strung out on drugs and sex. Men are marrying men. Marriages are ending in divorce.

The world is bombarded with hypocritical preachers, and the so-called church has attempted to pass itself off as the bride of Christ. The religion of the prostitute is based on the love of self.

The whore focuses on sex, money, and image. We live in a time of great despair, for this nation and the nations of the world have embraced a religion of perversion and hold to the practices of demons.

"For all nations have drunk of the wine of the wrath of her fornication, and the kings of the earth have committed fornication with her, and the merchants of the earth are waxed rich through the abundance of her delicacies. And I heard another voice from heaven, saying, Come out of her, my people, that ye be not partakers of

her sins, and that ye receive not of her plagues. For her sins have reached unto heaven, and God hath remembered her iniquities. And she shall be utterly burned with fire: for strong is the Lord God who judgeth her. And the kings of the earth, who have committed fornication and lived deliciously with her, shall bewail her, and lament for her, when they shall see the smoke of her burning" (Rev. 18:3–5, 8, 9). **God is calling His children to come out of her!** During this most trying time in the history of the world, the moral fiber of the country and of the world is showing the breast size of just about every woman who appears on television. The world has rejected the message of Jesus Christ for the latest tantalizing sex scandal.

During this time, the church has remained blatantly silent about scriptural issues concerning the family and the roles that God has established for us. The modern-day church has abandoned the most holy words of God and has adopted the perverse rhetoric of this worldly society. The modern church has led the way to the evilest time in the history of the world, for believers have not stood firm on God's Word. This false church is lukewarm. *"I know thy works, that thou art neither cold nor hot: I would thou wert cold or hot. So then because thou art lukewarm, and neither cold nor hot, I will spue thee out of my mouth. Because thou sayest, I am rich, and increased with goods, and have need of nothing; and knowest not that thou art wretched, and miserable, and poor, and blind, and naked" (Rev. 3:15–17).* Consequently, while the church was silent, husbands relinquished their roles as providers. Wives went to work, and abandoned their roles as mothers. The family then came under attack from Satan, and the institution of marriage was perverted. The whore should be ashamed, but ashamed she is not, for she is the tool of Satan and is void of God's Spirit. *"For Jesus said unto Simon, son of Jonas (which is Peter), Do you love me more than man? And Peter answered, Yes, Lord; thou knowest that I love thee. Jesus said, Feed my lambs. Jesus asked Peter a second time, Do you love me? And Peter said, Master, you know I love you. Jesus said, Feed my sheep. Jesus asked for the third time, Peter, do you love me? And Peter was saddened, for Christ had asked him for a third time, and Peter said, Lord, you know if I love you, for you know everything, and you know that I love you! Then Jesus replied, Feed my sheep"* (John 21:15–17, author's paraphrase). "Woe be unto the pastors that destroy and scatter the sheep of my pasture! saith the Lord" (Jer. 23:1).

When pastors do not preach or teach God's full message, they are perverting the true message. When you cannot depend on the pastor of the modern-day church to tell you the truth, you should know that the end is drawing near. The modern-day church has forsaken the infallible Word of God for the fading acceptance of a dying world. The role of the true Church of Jesus Christ is to proclaim the gospel, live according to His Word under the guidance of His precious Holy Spirit, and to not compromise His Word. It does not matter if society has changed. The Word of God has remained the same throughout the history of the world. God is sovereign. He does not conform to our desire; we conform to His desire and to His Word.

We have entered into uncharted and dangerous waters. The modern-day church has led the way to these perilous times. The Bible says that in the last days, men and women will gather themselves teachers and preachers to tell them what they want to hear (2 Tim. 4:3–4). The church has become a place of perversion and hypocrisy and is leading this generation to a head-on confrontation with God. I do not perceive those in authority in the pulpits of America or throughout the world changing their message to help you. Too much financial and material gain is to be made. The change must come from us if we are going to be in compliance with God's Word.

I would like to pose the following questions. Do we believe that Jesus Christ is almighty God who came down from heaven, took on an earthly body, and died for the sins of His people? Do we believe that He rose from the grave on the third day, having all power in His hand? If we truly believe and are called according to His purpose, we can live victoriously in Christ Jesus. We are without excuse, for we have entered into the knowledge of the truth. *"Therefore to him that knoweth to do good, and doeth it not, to him it is sin" (James 4:17).* I know this is a tough pill to swallow, but we have been set up by wolves in sheep's clothing and led down a perverse and wicked path that is leading to our destruction. We have spiritually bought into a false and wicked doctrine, which destroys families, perverts the gospel, effeminizes women, and emasculates men. *"Now the Spirit speaketh expressly, that in the latter times some shall depart from the faith, giving heed to seducing spirits, and doctrines of devils" (1 Tim. 4:1). "And with all deceivableness of unrighteousness in them that perish; because they received not the love of the truth, that they might be saved. And for this cause God shall send them strong delusion, that they should believe a lie: That they all might be damned who believed not the truth, but had pleasure in unrighteousness" (2 Thess. 2:10–12).*

We who know the truth of God's Word must not be silent. We must resist the temptations of the devil. For the Word of God says: *"Be ye not unequally yoked together with unbelievers: for what fellowship hath righteousness with unrighteousness? and what communion hath light with darkness? And what concord hath Christ with Belial [the wicked]? or what part hath he that believeth with an infidel? And what agreement hath the temple of God with idols? for ye are the temple of the living God; as God hath said, I will dwell in them, and walk in them; and I will be their God, and they shall be my people. Wherefore come out from among them, and be ye separate, saith the Lord and touch not the unclean thing; and I will receive you. And will be a Father unto you, and ye shall be my sons and daughters, saith the Lord Almighty" (2 Cor. 6:14–18).*

My friends, the traditional, corporate, or whatever-you-want-to-call-it church is not preaching the unadulterated gospel of Jesus Christ! The Bible says, *"Ye shall know them by their fruits" (Matt. 7:16)*. All you have to do is observe and see what the church produces. Our wives and our daughters have been encouraged to work outside of the home, to live lives of promiscuity, to have children without husbands, and to be led away and deceived into all sorts of diverse perversions.

It is a sad state of affairs when you walk into a typical church and the pastor is preaching a political or sociological message, while his congregation is dying from spiritual starvation. The Prophet Amos prophesied that the day would come when a famine would be in the land—not one of food or water, but of hearing the Word of God. Young men and women would look all over for the true Word of God and not find it. Therefore they will fall by the wayside and falter. The time that Amos had prophesized about is here today. Our salvation is not in the traditional man-made church, but in the Word of God, which is the Spirit of Jesus Christ.

The Apostle Paul wrote, *"How then shall they call on him in whom they have not believed? and how shall they believe in him of whom they have not heard? and how shall they hear without a preacher? And how shall they preach, except they be sent?" (Rom. 10:14–15)*. My friends, many people are calling themselves preachers who are not. They carry the title of pastor for their own personal gain. One day an older preacher said unto me these words: "Son, some preachers were called, some were sent, and some just plain old went." We have a lot of so-called preachers whom God never called to preach the gospel, but they still went out on their own, many for their own material gain.

So you may ask, what are we to do? How will we ever know the truth? And I would reply that the Bible says that true worshipers of God will worship Him in Spirit and in truth (John 4:23–24). It is your responsibility to study the Word of God (2 Tim. 2:15). Men, you have the responsibility to teach your wives and families the truth about God's Word (1 Cor. 14:34–35). You cannot depend on anyone to tell you the truth about God's Word. You must know the Word for yourself (2 Tim. 2:15).

This is a sad time that we are living in. Many false prophets are in the world among us, and they have received their mission from their father, which is the devil. In 2 Thessalonians chapter 2, the Lord warned us through the Apostle Paul that Satan, that man of perdition, would sit in the temple of God, portraying himself as God. Satan has entered into the souls of the tares, which are the unbelievers, and has used a great delusion to fool the inhabitants of the world that his tares are the wheat. But the wheat are the elect of God whom Satan cannot have. Therefore, if you cannot trust those who call themselves pastors to preach God's true Word, then you must ask yourself why.

The answer is quite simple: Satan hates you, and will pervert the message of Jesus Christ to destroy you.

When Satan comes in to your home, he attempts to do four things:

1. Pervert and modernize your mindset to compromise the Word of God for your own fleshly desires.
2. Convince you how unfair God is toward you concerning His sovereign will.
3. Cause you to act out your perversion by being in rebellion to God's Word.
4. Destroy your marriage, defile your children, and ruin your fellowship with God.

Many false religions today look at the so-called "Christian" church and laugh at its ineffectiveness. The church is ineffective because it has forsaken the true Word of God.

What this book will attempt to do is to address some of the false doctrines that have been promoted by this false bride. God is calling unto us to "come out from among her and be ye separate!" Repent and ask God for forgiveness! The stench of mankind's sin has reached heaven, and God is not pleased!

Chapter Two:

Do You Sweat?
The Fall of Man

♛

For us to understand God's will for our lives and the importance of being obedient to the Word of God, we must go back to the beginning of time and explore the magnitude of the fall of man. Genesis 3:6–13 describes the fall and judgment of man. Genesis 3:17–19 details how God instituted the curse upon man. The curse that God placed upon man is that he should work and labor from the sweat of his brow all the days of his life. *"And unto Adam he said, Because thou hast hearkened unto the voice of thy wife, and hast eaten of the tree, of which I commanded thee, saying, Thou shalt not eat of it: cursed is the ground for thy sake; in sorrow shalt thou eat of it all the days of thy life; Thorns also and thistles shall it bring forth to thee; and thou shalt eat the herb of the field; In the sweat of thy face shalt thou eat bread, till thou return unto the ground; for out of it wast thou taken: for dust thou art, and unto dust shalt thou return."* God instituted the curse because of Adam's sin in the Garden of Eden. However, man was not the only one who was cursed. The Bible tells us that the serpent that Satan inhabited was cursed also, for he had deceived Eve. Because of the serpent's deception, it was cursed to crawl on its belly and eat the dust of the earth all the days of its life. God then told Eve (the woman) that her sorrow would be increased and that she would labor in pain while giving birth to her children. God also mandated that the woman's desire would be to please her husband and to submit unto him. *"Unto the woman he said, I will greatly multiply thy sorrow and thy conception; in sorrow thou shalt bring forth children; and thy desire shall be to thy husband, and he shall rule over thee"* (Gen. 3:16).

The reason God told Eve that her desire should be toward her husband is that God recognized that this was not Eve's (a woman's) desire. She craved for knowledge and worldly acceptance. I would like to pose a simple question. Are you, your mother, your wife, or your daughter taking on Adam's curse? Some may not understand what is meant by this question, so I will try to be direct. Do we crawl on the ground eating the dust of the earth? The answer is no! This was neither our burden nor our curse. This curse belongs to the serpent. This next question I will pose to the men. Do we have pain when we give birth to children? Of course we don't; this was neither our burden nor our curse, for God placed this on the woman.

This next question is to the women. Do you labor in the workforce with the sweat coming off your brow, working forty or more hours a week? Sadly to say, many will answer yes. However, the question you need to be asking yourself is why? Why are you placing yourself under the curse of man? I realize that many single mothers are placed in situations where they must work. However, there are still damaging consequences for participating in the curse of man. I will thoroughly detail these consequences later on in this book. When I observe today's family structure, I become upset in my spirit. Because the fact is that many churches, ministers, pastors, and all those who claim to be holy have remained deadly silent concerning the curse of man. This curse can help lead to the destruction of the family when the wife partakes in it. Please understand what I am attempting to say. The family is perverted when the woman works outside of the home under the authority and leadership of someone else. What do you think the apostles would think of today's unscriptural practice?

Would they condone married women working outside of the home under the supervision of someone other than their husbands as they become their families' providers? Would they understand that we live in the twenty-first century and that times and cultures change?

Or do you believe that they would confront today's men and ask them why they would place their curse on their wives and daughters? If God's Word (the Bible) is meant for today's generation, then many families throughout the world are in direct conflict with the Word of God. In 1 Timothy 2:11–15, the Lord takes family responsibility very seriously. God notices the way a woman cares for her children and manages her household. A wife's diligence in caring for her family clearly indicates her faithfulness to God.

The Bible says in Titus 2:5 that when men and women disobey God's commandments, we blaspheme His Word. Many today believe that we as a society have moved past the old outdated doctrines of the Bible. In today's society, the modern-day church has given many women a different message from what is in the Bible. Women who have husbands and children are now given the option to work and pursue their careers and to leave the raising of their children to nannies, babysitters, or childcare providers. Paul wrote in his letter to Titus, *"The aged women likewise, that they be in behaviour as becometh holiness, not false accusers, not given to much wine, teachers of good things; That they may teach the young women to be sober, to love their husbands, to love their children, To be discreet, chaste, keepers at home, good, obedient to their own husbands, that the word of God be not blasphemed (Titus 2:3–5).* Would it surprise anyone that man in his hypocritical self-determination has placed his curse on females? I certainly understand why God says that the very thoughts of an unsaved man are wicked and his ways are continually evil.

"And God saw that the wickedness of man was great

in the earth, and that every imagination of the thoughts of his heart was only evil continually" (Gen. 6:5). *"For out of the heart proceed evil thoughts, murders, adulteries, fornications, thefts, false witness, blasphemies"* (Matt. 15:19). This generation of men will defy God's Word for what they desire. However, the Bible says to seek God first! *"But seek ye first the kingdom of God, and his righteousness; and all these things shall be added unto you" (Matt. 6:33)*. Nevertheless, we send our wives to work because we want those materialistic things in life. The wife is mandated by God to submit herself only unto her husband. However, we are placing our wives under submission to someone else at work. *"Wives, submit yourselves unto your own husbands, as unto the Lord. For the husband is the head of the wife, even as Christ is the head of the church: and he is the saviour of the body" (Eph. 5:22–23)*. *"Wives, submit yourselves unto your own husbands, as it is fit in the Lord" (Col. 3:18)*. *"But I would have you know, that the head of every man is Christ; and the head of the woman is the man; and the head of Christ is God" (1 Cor. 11:3)*.

If you believe the Bible is outdated and not for sound doctrine in this modern world, you will simply ignore those Scriptures and the very content of this book. However, if you are a true *Bible*-believing Christian, you cannot ignore or explain away these Scriptures. God has made the roles of wives and husbands very clear. He also made it quite clear that work is a curse given unto man (Gen. 3:17). Consequently, when a wife works outside of the home and takes on the role of provider, she partakes in the curse. Thus the family is destined to receive the consequences of the curse. *"The aged women likewise, that they be in behaviour as becometh holiness, not false accusers, not given to much wine, teachers of good things; That they may teach the young women to be sober, to love their husbands, to love their children, To be discreet, chaste, keepers at home, good, obedient to their own husbands, that the word of God be not blasphemed" (Titus 2:3–5).* However, those who sit in the pulpits of America have kept silent. They have encouraged and even promoted this doctrine of women working and leaving their homes and their children.

When we look at today's family, it has been perverted. The modern-day church has watered down the gospel of Jesus Christ. His message has been perverted for the materialistic gain of having women work. *"Heaven and earth shall pass away, but my words shall not pass away" (Matt. 24:35).* Today's modern church has influenced many to accept this doctrine of women working outside of the home. *"Be not deceived; God is not mocked: for whatsoever a man soweth, that shall he shall also reap" (Gal. 6:7).* When we attempt to change the family structure and the format that God has put in place, we set ourselves up to be in direct conflict with God's ultimate plan for our lives. We must accept His full Word and not deviate from it. *"For I testify unto every man that heareth the words of the prophecy of this book, If any man shall add unto these things, God shall add unto him the plagues that are written in this book:*

And if any man shall take away from the words of the book of this prophecy, God shall take away his part out of the book of life, and out of the holy city, and from the things which are written in this book" (Rev. 22:18–19).

My brothers, do you realize that when our wives work outside of the home she places herself under the authority of someone else? However, the Bible says that the head of the wife is the husband and that the wife should be under submission only to him. *"Wives, submit yourselves unto your own husbands, as unto the Lord. For the husband is the head of the wife, even as Christ is the head of the church: and he is the saviour of the body. Therefore as the church is subject unto Christ, so let the wives be to their own husbands in **every thing**" (Eph. 5:22–24, emphasis added).*

When the wife works outside of the home under the authority of someone else and takes on the role of provider, she becomes submissive. The boss is now the head of your household, and your wife is obligated to listen to him whether she likes it or not. I have witnessed many supervisors mandate a dress code to their female employees. They will tell them how to dress, what to wear, and how to wear it. The boss in essence is the head of the household. The working wife will get up out of her bed so that she can be at work at the time required by her boss. Many husbands have unknowingly encouraged their wives to place themselves under the submission of another person.

We must realize that when the wife returns home from work, she is not the same as when she left. She has been spiritually compromising herself. She has been submitting eight hours a day to her boss to help support the family. She is often tired and unable to perform her God-ordained duties as a mother to her children and wife to her husband. Some of the results of the curse can be directly attributed to the high divorce rate, teenage pregnancy, and the rampant increase of marital infidelity. When a woman works outside of her home under the authority of someone other than her husband, Satan has room to operate and to cause division within the household, for the household is not in accordance with the Word of God. The Apostle Paul wrote that women are to be *"discreet, chaste, keepers at home, good, obedient to their own husbands, that the word of God be not blasphemed" (Titus 2:5).*

Sadly, we find that many of today's single mothers have no other option but to work outside of the home, for if they do not work, their children will not eat. Nevertheless, even if this is the case, the woman is still placing herself and her children under the curse of man. Some may feel that God has mercy on the women who work and provide for their families, and I would not disagree. Yet the curse will still manifest itself when the woman leaves her children under the care and authority of someone else while she is at work. This will expose her child to different teachings and abnormal maternal nurturing, which is one of the ramifications of the curse of man.

Remember that your child is yours—not the nanny's or the babysitter's, but yours. If you must sacrifice your career so that you could be obedient to God and raise your own children, then where is the sacrifice? If you find your fleshly life in this world, you will lose your spiritual life in the world to come (John 12:25). God has ordained that you submit yourself to His Word, and not unto the word of a man. *"This know also, that in the last days perilous times shall come. For men shall be lovers of their own selves, covetous, boasters, proud, blasphemers, disobedient to parents, unthankful, unholy, Without natural affection, trucebreakers, false accusers, incontinent, fierce, despisers of those that are good, Traitors, heady, highminded, lovers of pleasures more than lovers of God; Having a form of godliness, but denying the power thereof: from such turn away"* (2 Tim. 3:1–5).

Many husbands and wives are unaware of God's ultimate plan for the Christian family. If this is your situation, God is calling unto the husband to take the leadership role and make provisions for his wife so that she can stop working away from her home and children. My brother, stand in the gap for your wife and family. It is time to free your wife from labor as a provider and enter into the knowledge of God's divine Word. It is up to you to provide for your family and to lead your wife as the head of your household. If you cannot afford your house without the help of your wife's salary, then move to a house that you can afford on your own. We must be in compliance with God's Word. Your wife should not be working outside of the home under the authority of someone else. It is not her responsibility to take on your curse. *"But if any provide not for his own, and specially for those of his own house, he hath denied the faith, and is worse than an infidel. I will therefore that the younger women marry, bear children, guide the house, give none occasion to the adversary to speak reproachfully"* (1 Tim. 5:8, 14).

This reminds me of a time when I was listening to my radio to a preacher from Dallas, Texas, who was telling his parishioners that a woman can work outside of the home as long as it does not interfere with her duties as a wife and mother. I agree somewhat with this statement but only for women who own their own businesses and are not under submission to anyone except their husbands if married. The woman who is self-employed has more independence and autonomy than the typical working mother and wife.

However, if she is married, she should be under the leadership of her husband. The woman who owns her own business is not under the authority of someone else, for she has unquestioned latitude and flexibility to attend to her family's needs. Then there are those wives who work for ministries or Christian schools that help mentor, educate, teach, and train our children. If you participate in a Bible-believing ministry or a fellowship that promotes a family-first philosophy consistent with Scripture, this would be an acceptable alternative. Nevertheless, the ideal biblically based situation would be that the wife remains home, administrates her home, and volunteers at her local fellowship or ministry. The stay-at-home mom has the authority to leave and to go wherever and whenever she pleases without any ramifications of her time being usurped by anyone other than her husband. Then the wife is not placing the family in jeopardy of the curse. The curse only takes affect if it's Adam-type work. For example, working out of necessity and under someone else's authority places you under the curse of Adam. It takes you away from your first priority, which is your family.

Who can find a virtuous woman? for her price is far above rubies. The heart of her husband doth safely trust in her, so that he shall have no need of spoil. She will do him good and not evil all the days of her life. She seeketh wool, and flax, and worketh willingly with her hands. She is like the merchants' ships; she bringeth her food from afar. She riseth also while it is yet night, and giveth meat to her household, and a portion to her maidens. She considereth a field, and buyeth it: with the fruit of her hands she planteth a vineyard. She girdeth her loins with strength, and strengtheneth her arms. She perceiveth that her merchandise is good: her candle goeth not out by night. She layeth her hands to the spindle, and her hands hold the distaff. She stretcheth out her hand to the poor; yea, she reacheth forth her hands to the needy. She is not afraid of the snow for her household: for all her household are clothed with scarlet. She maketh herself coverings of tapestry; her clothing is silk and purple. Her husband is known in the gates, when he sitteth among the elders of the land. She maketh fine linen, and selleth it; and delivereth girdles unto the merchant. Strength and honour are her clothing; and she shall rejoice in time to come. She openeth her mouth with wisdom; and in her tongue is the law of kindness. She looketh well to the ways of her household, and eateth not the bread of idleness. Her children arise up, and call her blessed; her husband also, and he praiseth her. Many daughters have done virtuously, but thou excellest them all. Favour is deceitful, and beauty is vain: but a woman that feareth the Lord, she shall be praised. Give her of the fruit of her hands; and let her own works praise her in the gates. (Prov. 31:10–31)*

My friends, the virtuous woman is an example of many things; however, the main purpose of this story is to give a clear depiction of what God considers a holy and righteous Christian woman. As we observe this story, we can see that this was a hard-workingwoman! She did a lot of work for her family, and sought the approval of her husband, as she was carrying out her daily duties.

This parable is consistent with Scripture, for she was not beholden to anyone but her husband. This afforded her the opportunity to care for her children, which is consistent with Scripture. She also provided additional monies to the household budget by working, but only under her own authority or her husband's. For the Lord desires that the woman make her family her first priority. *"That they may teach the young women to be sober, to love their husbands, to love their children, To be discreet, chaste, keepers at home, good, obedient to their own husbands, that the word of God be not blasphemed" (Titus 2:4–5)*. But the bottom line is this: If you are a mother or a wife and you are still working outside of the home, your family is under the curse of man and will certainly receive the results of the curse. The husband should do all he can to help get his wife and himself out of this predicament.

I realize that this is a difficult concept to accept, for we certainly live in perilous times where men and women have accepted the perverse doctrines of Satan. Many men and women would rather please their lustful desires than serve God. Many have abandoned the life to come through Jesus Christ for the worldly pleasures of today. However, the Bible says, *"He that loveth his life shall lose it; and he that hateth his life in this world shall keep it unto life eternal. If any man serve me, let him follow me; and where I am, there shall also my servant be: if any man serve me, him will my Father honour" (John 12:25–26).* God has not decreed for the wife to be under submission to anyone except her husband and ultimately unto God.

"Unto the woman he said, I will greatly multiply thy sorrow and thy conception; in sorrow thou shalt bring forth children; and thy desire shall be to thy husband, and he shall rule over thee" (Gen. 3:16). "Wives, submit yourselves unto your own husbands, as unto the Lord. For the husband is the head of the wife, even as Christ is the head of the church: and he is the saviour of the body. Therefore as the church is subject unto Christ, so let the wives be to their own husbands in every thing" (Eph. 5:22–24). It is the responsibility of a man to provide for his wife and family, and if he does not, he is worse than

an infidel. *"But if any provide not for **his** own, and specially for those of **his** own house, **he** hath denied the faith, and is worse than an infidel" (1 Tim. 5:8, emphasis added).* The word "infidel" is taken from the word "infidelity," which means unbelief in God's revelation. This is a horrible predicament to be in.

We as a people must ask ourselves this question: Are we Bible-believing Christians or corporate Christians? Believe me, there is a huge difference. When I look at this present generation of men, I see infidels and unbelievers in God's revelation. From the beginning of time, God had forewarned us about a generation of people who would have a form of godliness but deny His power, which is His Word. My friends, we live in that generation today. Infidels are all around us. For the Bible says, *"The gate to hell is wide and the road is broad that leadeth into destruction, and many will enter in; but straight is the gate and narrow is the way which leadeth into life, and few are those that find it"* (Matt. 7:13–14, author's paraphrase).

My brothers, we must work hard to keep our wives out of Adam's curse. For the Lord has revealed unto us the knowledge of our curse and the ramifications it will have on our families. We should no longer wonder why the children of today are strung out on drugs and alcohol. This is why many parents find themselves having to put their daughters on birth control and to teach their sons how to use condoms. Their minds have been strung out on sex. Our children have been spiritually perverted because women have entered into a curse with the backing of their fathers, husbands, preachers, and teachers. Juvenile crime is running rampant, marriages are ending in divorce, and homes are left destitute. Christians, wake up!

Stop selling out God. *"Remember therefore from whence thou art fallen, and repent, and do the first works" (Rev. 2:5).* *"Preach the word; be instant in season, out of season; reprove, rebuke, exhort with all long suffering and doctrine" (2 Tim. 4:2).*

Chapter Three:

The Auction Block

An auction block is a place where merchandise is bought and sold to the highest bidder. Those who participate in the bidding process are usually invited guests who are deemed to be financially worthy and have distinguished themselves within the local community. However, anyone who is considered eligible could participate in this process.

During the height of slavery, auctions were used to sell slaves to the highest bidders. Auction-block bidding was a very important event for slave owners. This was when a master could buy a big, strong, Negro man to tend the fields or a well-mannered houseboy to keep his big house clean. It was a time of great anxiety for the slave owners. Many found themselves competing

The Prostitute in the Pulpit

and bidding against one another. The purchase of a strong, dependable slave could earn a master untold material profit.

The auctioneer usually facilitated the bidding process. He was empowered by the owner of the auction to negotiate, mediate, and garner the best prices for the merchandise. The auctioneer represented the interest of international slave traders, and his job was to negotiate a price that would best benefit his clients.

The most exciting time would come when the women would be paraded on the auction block. Men would come from many miles away to bid on the young, healthy-looking Negro slave girls. The auctioneer would normally entice the crowd by parading these young slave girls up to the auction block barely dressed, if they were dressed at all, with their hands tied behind their backs. He would then begin to maneuver himself all over the young slave girl's body. He would also carry what we call today a pointer stick. He would use the stick to point out to the bidders the various well-endowed areas that some would possibly find appealing. The auctioneer would unveil the slave's breasts, vagina, buttocks, teeth, eyes, tongue, feet, and anything else the bidders requested to see. Once the bidding began, it was fast and furious. The testosterone levels in the crowd would usually reach fever pitch.

Once the bidding process was complete, the slave owner who bid the highest price would take possession of his new prized slave. Once the slave master had officially gained custody of his property, he would place his

The Auction Block

mark on the slave. He had cart-blanche access to his new personal slave girl. He could do things to this slave girl that he wouldn't dare think about doing with his wife. Whenever the master wanted sex, all he had to do was call for his little black slave, and she would prepare herself for his arrival. When the slave girl met a fellow male slave, and they decided to "jump the broom," which constituted marriage for the slave, the master would still exhibit his authority and ownership of those slaves. It would not be a strange occurrence for the slave master to walk into the couple's shack and order the male slave out. The black male normally had a demeaning name such as "Cornbread." The slave master would then proceed to rape this young bride in front of her new groom. The master would place his will on this young woman to remind her that she was his nigger and that her husband was nothing but a boy. These types of acts stood as a reminder to the slaves that he was the master who bought them on the auction block. The young slave girl was nothing but his prostitute, and if she ever forgot that fact, he had his ways to remind her.

My friends, words cannot describe the evilness of this practice. This was certainly a black eye on American and world history, and a wound that still lingers today.

Sadly, the auction block is alive and well. Many of today's husbands and wives have sold themselves spiritually for monetary and materialistic rewards. This type of slavery corrupts the mind and destroys the soul. It's a perversion of the Word of God!

This new form of slavery is used by Satan to entice

your flesh to have your spirit in bondage. Satan is the auctioneer. He has influenced the people of the world to deny the ultimate plan of God and to turn toward a doctrine of "me first." Women are now more concerned about their careers and ambitions. The time has now come that the Apostle Paul spoke about: *"This know also, that in the last days perilous times shall come. For men shall be lovers of their own selves, covetous, boasters, proud, blasphemers, disobedient to parents, unthankful, unholy" (2 Tim. 3:1–2).* The result of this mindset has left the family unit and the constitution of marriage in shambles. Consequently, the children are lacking what they need to live victoriously in this present time. Women are now preyed upon as easy victims for today's wayward men.

I have sat down and counseled many women who have looked for love and found lust. They found themselves looking for truth but discovered a lie. They searched for hope but found despair, for they searched without faith in God. Thus we find that welfare and social service agencies have attempted to take the place of the fathers that have abandoned their children. Consequently, today's women and young girls have been mistreated, abused, and then discarded by today's men. Oh, my friends, who can find a virtuous woman? God is calling for women to die to their fleshly desires, and be made alive to the Spirit of Jesus Christ. The world is in moral decay, for they have disobeyed the ultimate plan of God. Satan has deceived many women to parade themselves on the spiritual auction block, which

The Auction Block

has led to family confusion, separation, and ultimately toward sinful destruction.

Nevertheless, as in the days of slavery, if there were no owners of slaves, there could be no slavery. For slavery to exist, you must have slave owners. Sadly, however, today's modern-day husband has taken the role of the slave master. God has given him spiritual authority to lead and direct his family in the fear and admonition of the Lord. The husband will ultimately be held responsible for the collapse of his family, for God has called him to lead. The husband is the head of the wife and is responsible for her spiritual knowledge as well as her financial security.

I truly understand that many who read this book will vehemently reject it. However, you would not be rejecting my words but those that proceed from the Holy Scriptures. But if you wish to be ignorant, then by all means remain ignorant if this is your desire. For the Bible says, *"My people are destroyed for lack of knowledge: because thou hast rejected knowledge, I will also reject thee, that thou shalt be no priest to me: seeing thou hast forgotten the law of thy God, I will also forget thy children"* (Hos. 4:6). God will hold the husband responsible for not leading and teaching His infallible Word to his family. God held Adam responsible for Eve's disobedience in the garden. *"And unto Adam he said, Because thou hast hearkened unto the voice of thy wife, and hast eaten of the tree, of which I commanded thee, saying, Thou shalt not eat of it: cursed is the ground for thy sake; in sorrow shalt thou eat of it all the days of thy life" (Gen. 3:17). "And Adam was not deceived, but the woman being deceived was in the transgression" (1 Tim. 2:14).*

In the mid–1800's, there was an outcry from the people to abolish slavery. A group of people called the abolitionists spoke against the practice of slavery. Slavery divided this country, and helped bring forth the Civil War. My friends, today we need spirit-filled abolitionists, true Bible-believing Christian men and women who understand the plight of today's modern-day family. The path toward freedom has already been cleared. The Lord Jesus Christ has lit the path, and its direction leads to freedom. The directions to freedom are found in the holy map, which is the Bible. In the Bible you will find your freedom papers from the bondage of sin, and the call to depart from the false church (the great whore). Cry out to God and run to freedom, and let Him remove your shackles and deliver you from the chains of bondage, for you had been chosen before the foundation of the world.

Chapter Four:

Oh, America!

*I*n 1948, World War II ended with the surrender of Japan after the bombing of Hiroshima and Nagasaki, and the defeat of Germany led by the United States and her allies. When the war first began in December 1941 with the bombing of Pearl Harbor by the Japanese military, the United States military sent thousands of young men to war. As thousands of men left their wives and children at home to fight in the war, women went to work. Before this time, it was not the mainstream practice of this country for women to work outside of their homes and leave their children to be raised by others. Because of the evilness of war, women had little choice but to enter into the curse of man. However, after the war, many women decided they enjoyed the taste of working and being independent from their husbands. It was soon after the war that the feminist movement began. One of the most destructive objectives of the women's movement was to be like men. The feminist movement expressed its dissatisfaction of being women in America in several different ways. One way was to burn bras in the middle of the streets to help bring attention and protest the discrimination that this country had shown toward women. Throughout the late 1960's and early 1970's, young people of that time revolted against the mainstream doctrinal practices of the American culture. They were referred to as "flower children" and the "baby-boomer generation." This generation of men and women declared unto the world, "If it feels good, do it."

Many women made conscious decisions to openly deny the ultimate plan of God for their independence and self-gratification. The daughters of the bra-burning revolution are the offspring of the wartime working women. Obviously many of the parents of that generation passed on a doctrine of self-gratification and self-fulfillment to their children. Consequently, the children of the war were raised with the concept of women working outside of the home, embracing the curse of Adam. The results of this teaching, I believe, gave birth to a new people and a different generation called "Generation X."

The curse of having women work outside of their home and away from their children has been taught, encouraged, and proclaimed by presidents, preachers, and teachers. However, more importantly, our Lord and

Savior Jesus Christ has not proclaimed it. For the Bible says that it is the husband's duty and responsibility to provide for his children and his wife. The wife's responsibility is to take care of her family, be the administrator of the home, and train and raise the children. The wife is also called to teach young women to be holy and respectful young ladies. *"But if any provide not for his own, and specially for those of his own house, he hath denied the faith, and is worse than an infidel. I will therefore that the younger women marry, bear children, guide the house, give none occasion to the adversary to speak reproachfully. For some are already turned aside after Satan" (1 Tim. 5:8, 14, 15).* This is God's proclamation to today's generation: repent and turn from your sins, for the Day of Judgment is at hand and is already at the door.

God has already set in place a system of how the family ought to function. If your parents raised you to believe that women should work outside of the home, they were wrong. If your husband tells you that you should work outside of the home, he's wrong. If the teachers and preachers in the modern-day church have told you that you should work outside of the home, they are lying and the truth is not in them. You have been going through life not understanding God's ultimate plan for the family.

The Lord has decreed for a woman to stay home, raise the children, and submit only unto her husband. I assume that you would like to be in compliance with God's Word. Do you understand that a curse is not a good thing? We must not think that God inspired men to write the Holy Scriptures for no reason. Think not that God's Word has no affect. **America is growing up cursed.** Women today do not need for the auctioneer to undress them. Women freely undress themselves and show their bodies to anyone who desires to look. This is a cursed behavior, inspired by women indulging in the curse of man. Women walk around half-naked so that they can get the attention of a man. You may ask why. Well, it's because they have been cursed. They have become perverted creatures, confused about what they really want out of life. Women have striven to become like man, and man is a wicked and perverse creature.

I understand what the flesh wants and desires, but if we are true Christians, we must die to the flesh and the evilness that it wants to do! *"For they that are after the flesh do mind the things of the flesh; but they that are after the Spirit the things of the Spirit. For to be carnally minded is death; but to be spiritually minded is life and peace. Because the carnal mind is enmity against God: for it is not subject to the law of God, neither indeed can be. So then they that are in the flesh cannot please God"* (Rom. 8:5–8). The flesh desires for you to be disobedient to God's Word. It finds no pleasure in the Spirit. If we are Christians, then we no longer live to the flesh, but we live according to the spirit. You may say that many people today are lying about their Christianity. I believe you would be correct in your assessment. *"And then will I profess unto them, I never knew you: depart from me, ye that work iniquity"* (Matt. 7:23). God expects His people to be in compliance with His Word, not by lip service, but by how we live our lives. *"Ye hypocrites, well did Esaias prophesy of you, saying, This people draweth nigh unto me with their mouth, and honoureth me with their lips; but their heart is far from me. But in vain they do worship me, teaching for doctrines the commandments of men" (Matt. 15:7–9).* We must search the Scriptures and be obedient unto them.

We have been led down the wrong side of the street. We have been fooled. We have been sold out and sold off to the highest bidder. We live in a sad time for women. Many women have been trained to think like men, to work outside of the home and pursue a curse. Oh, excuse me—a *career.* However, God clearly says in the Bible that a man should work all the days of his life and then die! *"Man goeth forth unto his work and to his labour until the evening" (Ps. 104:23). "In the sweat of thy face shalt thou eat bread, till thou return unto the ground; for out of it wast thou taken: for dust thou art, and unto dust shalt thou return" (Gen. 3:19).* This is God's desire. It is also God's desire that a woman administers her home, cares for her husband, and raises her children (Titus 2:3–5). This is the Word of God! If you don't like it, you have been exposed as a false Christian selling out God to fulfill your own unholy, unscriptural desires. *"He that loveth his life shall lose it; and he that hateth his life in this world shall keep it unto life eternal" (John 12:25). "And hereby we do know that we know him, if we keep his commandments. He that saith, I know him, and keepeth not his commandments, is a liar, and the truth is not in him. But whoso keepeth his word, in him verily is the love of God perfected: hereby know we that we are in him. He that saith he abideth in him ought himself also so to walk, even as he walked"* (1 John 2:3–6). We have been set up by wolves in sheep's clothing. The wolves are nothing but slave owners using you for their own gain.

They call you "friend" while they try to destroy your soul. The wolves are the ones who have placed us in this time of confusion. They have created a society where women would defy God's Word and try to take a curse and turn it into something good. They will pay young women money to take off their clothes. The wolves are the ones that created short dresses and high heels. They have turned your desire away from your husband and toward a man at your work place. **(The Boss!)** However, the Bible says that the wife's submission and desire should be for her husband. *"Wives, submit yourselves unto your own husbands, as it is fit in the Lord"* (Col. 3:18). *"Unto the woman he said, I will greatly multiply thy sorrow and thy conception; in sorrow thou shalt bring forth children; and thy desire shall be to thy husband, and he shall rule over thee"* (Gen. 3:16).

My friends, we have been fooled into living hypocritical, phony Christian lives. We call Jesus Lord, but we do not live according to His Word. *"Ye hypocrites, well did Esaias prophesy of you, saying, This people draweth nigh unto me with their mouth, and honoureth me with their lips; but their heart is far from me. But in vain they do worship me, teaching for doctrines* the commandments of men" (Matt. 15:7–9). Jesus describes Satan as a ravenous wolf prowling and searching for someone to devour. My friends, we have been preyed upon like sheep. The wolves have deceived us and have led us into their dens of sin.

Who are the wolves? Some would say that the preachers are the wolves, for they have turned many ears to false doctrines and many hearts away from the truth. *"These are wells without water, clouds that are carried with a tempest; to whom the mist of darkness is reserved for ever. For when they speak great swelling words of vanity, they allure through the lusts of the flesh, through much wantonness, those that were clean escaped from them who live in error. While they promise them liberty, they themselves are the servants of corruption: for of whom a man is overcome, of the same is he brought in bondage"* (2 Pet. 2:17–19). Some may say that the wolves are husbands who do not love their wives as Christ loves the true church (Eph. 5:22–33). Others would contend that the wolves are women who know the truth of God's Word, but continue to spiritually prostitute themselves for materialistic rewards. *"For it had been better for them not to have known the way of righteousness, than, after they have known it, to turn from the holy commandment delivered unto them"* (2 Pet. 2:21).

My friends, the wolves that attack the purity of God's Word are nothing but demons, which have crept in unaware trying to destroy the church of Jesus Christ. *"For there are certain men crept in unawares, who were before of old ordained to this condemnation, ungodly men, turning the grace of our God into lasciviousness, and denying the only Lord God, and our Lord Jesus Christ" (Jude 4).* The church is supposed to be a light to a dying world and an ambassador of the gospel. The twenty-third chapter of Jeremiah speaks on pastors who lead the sheep astray. Jesus had also told Peter to feed his sheep.

My friends, the wolves have made a grave mistake, for they have attempted to pervert the sheep of Jesus Christ. *"And when he putteth forth his own sheep, he goeth before them, and the sheep follow him: for they know his voice. And a stranger will they not follow, but will flee from him: for they know not the voice of strangers" (John 10:4–5).* The world has listened to strangers and liars behind the pulpit. They have tricked many to spiritually prostitute themselves for paychecks. The false church may have turned you into a whore, but Jesus can transform you into His bride. Jesus Christ has paid the price. *"In whom we have redemption through his blood, the forgiveness of sins, according to the riches of his grace" (Eph. 1:7).*

You are free from the master of this world. Jesus has taken you off the auction block. He paid for you through His blood. No one else could match His bid. Your name is no longer on the auction block of hell. Step down from your curse, for you have been set free!

Chapter Five:

The Betrayal!

The foundation of the family has always been predicated on the relationship of the husband and wife, which means a man and a woman. I'm sure most of you understood what I meant, but it's necessary to clarify what you're saying these days. God has ordained for this to be. However, we stand at a critical point in time where the sons of men have turned their backs on God! *"For the time will come when they will not endure sound doctrine; but after their own lusts shall they heap to themselves teachers, having itching ears; And they shall turn away their ears from the truth, and shall be turned unto fables" (2 Tim. 4:3–4).* "Men have become lovers of themselves rather than lovers of God" (2 Tim. 3:2–4, author's para-

phrase) Many men have tasted the wine of the world and forsaken the true wine given to us from our Master, Jesus Christ. Consequently, this leaves the woman with a perverted man. The daughters of men have always been enticed by evil and the sinful nature of men. "Why do good girls like bad boys?" Does that sound familiar? Women have been led astray and perverted by the waywardness of man.

The key to restoring Christ back into the family is through God's Word. Woman, if you have an unbelieving husband, he is sanctified through you if you are a believer. Man, if you have an unbelieving wife, she is sanctified through you if you are a believer (1 Cor. 7:14). What this means is that there is hope, because the spirit of Christ is present within the home. If the husband is not saved, the wife is instructed to show her holy and chaste behavior in front of her husband to hopefully have God show mercy on him and convert him (1 Cor. 7:16). Women are to pray for their husbands while being submissive unto them. *"Likewise, ye wives, be in subjection to your own husbands; that, if any obey not the word, they also may without the word be won by the conversation of the wives" (1 Pet. 3:1)*. I realize that it is very difficult to live with an unbelieving spouse. However, this was your decision—you married your mate, and God will hold you responsible to comply with His Word and to keep your vow.

Life is filled with burdens and temptations, and this generation has certainly entered into the snare of the serpent. As we have found throughout the history of

The Betrayal!

mankind, sin is contagious, for everybody has sin. Women have become accustomed to the curse of working like men. God is calling you out of this unscriptural masculine behavior. Why would you call Jesus your Lord and Savior when you do not do what He says? The problem we have today is that very few people want to tell anyone the truth. This is no surprise to God, for He is omniscient (He knows everything).

If you are married and if you and your spouse are believers, pray to God in the name of Jesus to help you comply with His Word. Many people will say that it takes two in today's society to just survive. That's a lie! It takes two to give you the type of lifestyle you desire. If you find your life in this world, you shall lose it in the life to come. But if you lose your life in this world for Jesus' sake, you shall gain eternal life (Matt. 10:38–39). It is very simple—if you love Jesus, you will pick up your cross, deny yourself, and follow Him. For what does it profit a man to gain the whole world and lose his soul in hell? (Matt. 16:26.)

Now is the time for the true believers of God to worship Him in spirit and in truth. Here is the truth: It was not the man who was deceived by Satan, but it was the woman; she encouraged her husband to disobey God (1 Tim. 2:13–14). Thus the man was cursed to work all the days of his life, and the woman would be under subjection to her husband (Gen. 3:16–19). For God created the man from the dust of the earth in His own image. The woman was created to be a companion and help for man (Gen. 2:7, 20–23). This is the natural truth.

Spiritually there is no difference between man and woman. We are all one in Christ Jesus (Gal. 3:28). However, my sisters, it was ordained from the time you left your mother's womb that you would be born in the flesh under submission to your husband. When you detour from God's purpose, you will incur His wrath. When we get to heaven, there will be neither male nor female, but we will be like the angels (Mark 12:24–25). Earth is only a temporary assignment, for we have a home in heaven not made by hands.

If you hear God's Word, please do not harden your heart, for God is trying to tell you something. Whatever you have to do to be in compliance with God's Word, do it! You may have to sell your home and move to a less expensive one. You may have to take your kids out of private school, or delay that vacation. Whatever has to be done, do it, for God is watching. Families are mandated by God to live on what the husband is able to provide (1 Tim. 5:8). True Christians are concerned with complying with God's Word and how they may please Him.

Many in the church and in the world will ignore this cry from the Spirit of God, but you, my friends, have tried God and you know that He is able. He's the faithful counselor, and his judgment is true. If a man does not lead or provide for his family, God has no part with him (1 Tim 5:8). The world has searched far and wide to try to make the Word of God obsolete. Time has continued to march on, and men have come and gone just like the wind, but God's Word continues to go on. My brothers, take your rightful place within your family. Women, take that bitterness out of your mouth, for God knows what you have been going through. Satan, we rebuke you in the name of Jesus. Women, we love you, for God has given you to us and we should love you as Christ loves the church (Eph. 5:25). When a man finds a Christian woman, he has found himself a good thing (Prov. 18:22). Women, take care of yourselves, conduct yourselves as Christian ladies, abstain from lowering yourselves to what the world expects from you, and hold on to God's image and His standards.

When you become involved in worldly activities and allow yourself to be defiled in immoral sexual misconduct, your spirit becomes as a harlot and a whore. Stop trying to be like men.

Society has perverted your thinking, for you have been told that if it is good for the goose, it's even better for the gander. Stop listening to the doctrine of demons (1 Tim. 4:1).

When a man and woman who aren't married have sex with one another, they become as one and are partakers of that spirit of perversion that only Jesus Christ can cleanse. Listen and understand what I am saying.

A woman can sleep with a hundred men and be classified as a loose woman, and rightfully so. However, our society has perverted this image for the man, for if he sleeps with a hundred women, he is classified as a ladies' man. This man's soul is just as corrupt as the woman's is. However, the nature of sin has corrupted the logic of man. A true Christian woman is precious in the sight of a Christian man (1 Cor. 11:7). When a woman conducts herself as God commanded, she is precious in His sight. My sisters, a true Christian man will admire your holy attitude and observe and respect your chaste behavior (Titus 2:4–5).

Chapter Six:

The Story of an Infidel

♛

*R*aising children is an awesome responsibility. I can recall that when our first daughter Breanna was born, my wife and I were very nervous. The responsibility of being parents seemed so complicated and so far above us. When the nurse informed me that it was time for my wife and Breanna to leave the hospital and go home, I thought she was joking. I said to the nurse, "Listen, I don't know what kind of operation you're running here, but it has been only three days since our baby was born, and you're putting her out already." Then my wife gently pulled me to the side and notified me that we had stayed longer than usual, and that it was now time to take Breanna home. I was very surprised to learn that most babies were released within forty-eight to seventy-two hours upon delivery. Recently, I have learned that this time has been reduced to twenty-four hours in most states. (Please bear with me while I digress.) Don't misinterpret what I'm trying to say. We were ecstatic about the birth of our first child. I had taken time off from work for those three days without pay and slept in the hospital room with my wife. Prior to the birth of our daughter, we were enrolled in Lamaze and other prenatal classes that were designed to help prepare us for the arrival of our child. We did very well in the Lamaze class. In fact, I was nicknamed "Mr. Lamaze," for I was the most enthusiastic of all the fathers. This was the most exciting time in our lives, for we were young and in love. Nevertheless, when the baby came, I suddenly realized that I was *unprepared!*

My parents were present with me at the hospital once Breanna was born, as well as my in-laws, who graciously imparted their wisdom, support, and advice. My sister-in-law was educating me on the joy of not circumcising the baby if it was a boy. My youngest brother came to the hospital, as well as a host of other family and friends. Yvonne and I had tremendous support, and still nothing could have prepared me for the awesomeness of being a parent. Everything seemed to hit me at once. The thought of providing food, shelter, clothing, and transportation seemed overwhelming. However, it didn't matter, for I was in love, and love would pull us through. Doesn't that sound romantic? *No. It was stupid!* I realized that I was unprepared, unskilled, immature, and in way over my head to take on the responsibility of a True Christian Husband and Father. Nevertheless, I had a wife who just went through labor and a newborn baby ready to call me "daddy." My family was in trouble, because they had to depend on me! I was scared for them, because my wife was the primary breadwinner and I was the one with the minimal paying job.

She had the benefits and I was still in college. I didn't know it at the time, but I was an *infidel,* and my wife was on the Auction Block. It's not what you say that declares your faith as a Christian. How you live determines who you are. The simple truth of the matter is that I was not a good candidate for marriage. I would venture to say that most marriages take place in ignorance of God's Word. I am happy to report that Breanna, who is now fifteen years old and the apple of her daddy's eye, is doing wonderfully. The Lord has also blessed Yvonne and me with our baby girl Candace, who is now twelve years old and is confident that she is Daddy's little baby. However, when Breanna and Candace were born, I can certainly testify that I was an infidel. My wife and children deserved more.

Our daughters, sisters, and mothers deserve more, and God demands more from a man when he marries a woman. The structure of the Christian family must conform to God's standards, and if it doesn't, it does not constitute a true Christian family. Our families have been living under a curse when our wives work outside of the home. The family unit has reaped the repercussions of the curse of man. This curse has ushered us in to the Generation of the Great Harlot. For we have spiritually prostituted our wives to work like men to provide for the family. The reason for this is quite simple: we live in the generation of the infidel.

God's judgment is upon this generation. It does not matter if you believe you are in God's will. The most important question is if God knows you. *"Not every one that saith unto me, Lord, Lord, shall enter into the kingdom of heaven; but he that doeth the will of my Father which is in heaven. Many will say to me in that day, Lord, Lord, have we not prophesied in thy name? and in thy name have cast out devils? and in thy name done many wonderful works? And then will I profess unto them, I never knew you: depart from me, ye that work iniquity" (Matt. 7:21–23).* According to the Scriptures, if a man allows a woman to work and take care of the family, he is worse than an infidel. *"But if any provide not for **his** own, and specially for those of **his** own house, **he** hath denied the faith, and is worse than an infidel" (1 Tim. 5:8, emphasis added).* I understand that many people will try to discount the Bible and say that it is outdated and not in touch with today's issues and the individuality of today's society. This self-serving idealistic attitude has been the launching pad for this sad, misdirected generation. Families are cursed when men forsake the very foundation of God's plan for the family. I thank God that I am aware of His Word and His plan for the Christian family.

Nevertheless, I was no better than an infidel; in fact, I was worse than an infidel, for I was ignorant of the charge that God placed at my feet. I was claiming to be a Christian minister and husband, but I was not living in accordance with His Word. I was never trained or taught by my parents, the church, or the Christian college I attended about the curse of Adam.

We have been set up to blatantly disavow God's Word because of a lack of strong biblical teaching.

I have wonderful parents. However, they depended on the preacher to teach them God's Word.

"Study to shew thyself approved unto God, a workman that needeth not to be ashamed, rightly dividing the word of truth" (2 Tim. 2:15). This is why it is so important for us to train our children now in the fullness of God's Word. *"Train up a child in the way he should go: and when he is old, he will not depart from it" (Prov. 22:6).* Our children have been left at home to raise themselves, and we wonder why we are cursed. Here is the basic truth: if we as parents raise our children up in the fear and knowledge of the Lord, they will respect our opinion on who is worthy to marry them. The Bible says, *"My people are destroyed for lack of knowledge: because thou hast rejected knowledge, I will also reject thee, that thou shalt be no priest to me: seeing thou hast forgotten the law of thy God, I will also forget thy children" (Hos. 4:6).* God has given us a blueprint to use for the institution of marriage. In Jewish customs during the patriarchal and monarchal periods, between Moses and Jesus, it was forbidden for children to marry without their parents' consent. It was commonly accepted that before the two

young people were betrothed to one another (engaged), a *ketubah,* which is a contract, had to be reached by the groom and the bride's father. The groom had to exhibit his spiritual purity to the father of the bride and prove that he had the financial means to provide and care for his daughter.

Also before they could officially be announced as engaged, a contract had to be signed by the groom and the bride's father stating that an agreement was reached and that the terms of the contract were acceptable. Once the contract (or in today's terminology, "prenuptial") was signed, the bride and groom were officially announced as engaged. This means that during this period, the groom was locked in for life to marry his bride. The only reason for dissolving this contract would be on the grounds of fornication. *"And I say unto you, Whosoever shall put away his wife, except it be for fornication, and shall marry another, committeth adultery: and whoso marrieth her which is put away doth commit adultery" (Matt. 19:9).* If no one commits fornication during the betrothal period, the couple is bound in marriage.

My friends, the church is engaged to Jesus Christ. He is the Bridegroom and the true church is His bride. The modern-day church represents the whore, for it perverts the truth. For us to be free from the bondage of death, we had to be bought with a price. Our Bridegroom, Jesus Christ, paid the price on Calvary's cross. Satan has no dominion over us any longer. He had ownership of us until Jesus paid the price. Jesus died so that we could have everlasting life. We were lost in our sins, and could not find our way until Jesus heard our cry and wiped our tears away. We as Christians have the same calling and responsibilities to submit unto Christ, as the wife is to submit unto her husband. However, the world, especially the United States, has severely altered and perverted God's plan. Consequently, this generation and the offspring of this generation have been set up to receive God's judgment. The Prostitute in the Pulpit has given birth to a wayward generation, which has embraced the curse of Adam. My friends, all you have to do is listen to the cries of the children and see how really cursed we are. Look at the bitterness of many women; they are destitute of the truth of God's Word.

Observe today's men—they take pleasure in pleasing their fleshly desires and have embraced the spirit of an infidel. Today's corporate church is predominately filled with women. The church depends on these women to keep its local assemblies afloat. Do you actually believe that these church leaders will tell their female parishioners to stop working and go home and raise their children? Of course not! Oh, you evil and wicked pastors, how will you escape the damnation of hell? Many are ignorant of God's Word, for they have chosen to believe a lie. God is not at fault if we choose to believe a lie. By nature, most mothers know that they should be home with their children. However, men and women have perverted themselves for the so-called American dream.

Women do not respect their husbands as Jesus commanded them to. Many young women claim they don't need men. Many say they are content with their own personal lifestyles and do not need husbands to validate their womanhood. In the book of 1 Corinthians, it states that you are better off if you did not marry, for you would be more available and able to serve the Lord as a single person. However, for those who desire marriage, God has given a blueprint on how to live. But the children of Satan have abandoned the marital blueprint that God has established. For these men and women who are willing to pervert God's plan and have set out to create their own plans—remember, you shall reap what you sow. You have compromised yourself, your spouse, and your children. *"For it had been better for them not to have known the way of righteousness, than, after they have known it, to turn from the holy commandment delivered unto them" (2 Pet. 2:21).* You have found pleasure in your sins, and tossed aside the holy words of God. For this, you are cursed. For you have found your life in this world, and chose to ignore the words of life that could have set you free.

No worldly job or man-made position is worth losing your soul in hell. Why would you do that? Men are sorry creatures destined for hell, unless we repent and call on the Lord Jesus Christ for His mercy. Jesus proposed marriage to the elect on Calvary's cross. He told us that He loved us and cared for us. He told us that we would have everything that He has. Eternal life is ours. This world is not our home, for the hands of men do not make our home. *"In my Father's house are many mansions: if it were not so, I would have told you. I go to prepare a place for you. And if I go and prepare a place for you, I will come again, and receive you unto myself; that where I am, there ye may be also" (John 14:2–3).* (What a husband!)

Jesus told us that he was going away to prepare a place for us, and that in His Father's house are many mansions. Jesus is preparing to take us home to claim us as His own. We are engaged to the Master and heirs to His throne. Jesus will introduce us to His Father and the angels will sing a song just for us. We will be married to the Master and heaven will be our home. Let us prepare for His coming, for we must get our house in order. We are the bride of Christ (the true church). The Scriptures tell us that salvation is a gift from God, so we do not have to work for our salvation. Jesus did all the work. Husbands, we are commanded to love our wives as Christ loves the church. The wife is mandated to depend on her husband for her physical and economic needs. If we call ourselves Christians, then we ought to obey the Word of the Lord!

Chapter Seven:

The Evil Eye!
What Are You Looking For?

A common battle cry of many women today is that there are no good men out there.

Some young women would say that all the good men are married. Others would say that most men have been in jail or have no job or are homosexual. The image that many women have of men today is very negative. The media and many talk shows have highlighted the negative and unwholesome side to many men of today. Statistics would seem to back up what many are saying about this current generation of men. Some of the more infamous negative characteristics of men are that they are dogs, wolves, players, and low-down cheats.

However, many women who hold to this perception

seem to be enticed by the physical and outward appearance of men. Often the traits that many worldly women see in a man are his clothes, the types of shoes he wears, or what kind of cologne he uses. Many women of today are overly concerned on how a man looks and how much money he makes. However, as a Christian young lady, your priorities should be contrary to those of worldly, unsaved women. If you noticed all of the traits just mentioned, you should realize that these are all predicated on the lust of the eyes and the desire of the flesh. *"For all that is in the world, the lust of the flesh, and the lust of the eyes, and the pride of life, is not of the Father, but is of the world" (1 John 2:16).* This should alarm many of you, for the fact is that many women, including so-called "Christian" women, are attracted to the same types of men. Isn't something wrong with this picture? *"For when we were in the flesh, the motions of sins, which were by the law, did work in our members to bring forth fruit unto death. For I know that in me (that is, in my flesh,) dwelleth no good thing: for to will is present with me; but how to perform that which is good I find not" (Rom. 7:5, 18).*

As Christians, we are supposed to be dead to our flesh and alive in God's spirit. The things that a Christian woman would look for should be opposite of a worldly woman. Nevertheless, many women who claim Jesus Christ as their personal savior continue to marry unsaved, worldly-minded men. This is why we have so many women attending the false church by themselves. They have married unsaved non-Bible-believing men, and now find themselves crying out to God for marital peace. Many women later realize they married according to the flesh and not according to the Spirit, all because the men looked good! You may try to deny it, but the truth is the truth.

If you want a Christian man, conduct yourself in a Christian manner. A worldly woman does not want a guy who reads his Bible, says his prayers, and is in the house by 9:00 p.m. (Men like this are still out there!) However, as those who live in the world will tell you, most parties do not begin until after midnight. A lot of the so-called "Christian" young women have become partakers in this type of lifestyle. Many refuse to even date or speak to a man unless he has money or is enticing to the eye. I can recall early in my ministry that a young lady at my church asked me why she could not go to a dance club. She stated that the pastor drinks alcohol and supplies alcoholic beverages to other church members as well. She then went on to say that many of the deacons drink and dance at the club, so why couldn't she. I would not, nor could not, defend the pastor's or deacon's behavior. However, the flesh is always looking for a way to get around God's Word.

This young woman wanted to do what her flesh wanted her to do. We are either for God or against Him; there is no middle ground. If you are a Christian young woman, then act like it. We are called to conduct ourselves as God has set forth in His Word. Therefore, call unto the Lord and pray that He will develop a fellowship of believers so that you can assemble with them.

I know it may be difficult, but pray for God's guidance. Be careful whom you associate with, for evil communication will cause you to fall. *"Be not deceived: evil communications corrupt good manners" (1 Cor. 15:33).* God cares about your wellbeing; reflect and realize God's love for you. Stop sleeping around, for you are defiling your soul. You are precious in the sight of God! If you love Christ Jesus, let your light shine unto the world, for the Christian is the salt of the earth and a light of hope to a dying and lost world.

Many men and women have sold their souls to the devil. The daughters of men have become defiled by the perversion of the world. Children today discuss sex openly and are irresponsible. Many public school systems have become inundated with teenage pregnancy and illegal drug use. Many people have stated that it takes a village to raise a child. I'm sorry, but this is not true. It takes the power of the Holy Spirit to raise your child within this sinful village of the world. It is not a strange occurrence within our society to have children having sex with one another. As a matter of fact, many schools and churches distribute condoms to school-age boys and girls. The main reason this is happening is because women have entered into the curse of Adam.

Women give many reasons for working outside of the home. Some women would say that they have no choice. Many may say that their husbands don't or won't work. Or if they do work, they won't share their earnings with their families. Some women say that their husbands do not make enough money to support their families, while others do not trust or want to rely on their husbands for their financial stability. Consequently, no matter what reason is given, the wife is entering into the curse of man and the family will reap the results of the curse. Women give various reasons for leaving their homes and children to the care of others. Some desire to be independent women who refuse to rely on their husbands for their financial well-being.

Then we have women who are the victims of divorce. The husband may leave his wife with no financial means for survival. I believe the only valid reason for a woman to work like Adam is if her husband divorces or separates from her. When a man leaves his wife, he causes her to enter the curse, which leaves her financially destitute. In this situation, a woman is placed in a cursed position, which is through no fault of her own. For example, sadly to say, the world today is not the safest place for a woman. Many women have been beaten, raped, or sexually abused. If a woman is raped, technically she had sexual intercourse with her attacker. Does this mean that she committed fornication, or if married, has committed adultery with her attacker? Of course not! These women have been taken advantage of and defiled against their will. When a husband demands that his wife work outside of the home under the authority of someone other than himself, he is allowing the curse of man to spiritually rape her. Consequently, he is forcing his wife to go against the plan of God. And when this happens, the family is torn apart, and the woman is defiled. Therefore, the children are raising themselves at home without the nurturing guidance of their mother.

Many mothers have sold out their children for their own personal so-called career. We are certainly living in the last days, for men and women would rather do for themselves than for their children! *"This know also, that in the last days perilous times shall come. For men shall be lovers of their own selves, covetous, boasters, proud, blasphemers, disobedient to parents, unthankful, unholy, Without natural affection, trucebreakers, false accusers, incontinent, fierce, despisers of those that are good, Traitors, heady, highminded, lovers of pleasures more than lovers of God" (2 Tim. 3:1–4)*. My friends, just because it seems as though the world does not obey God's Word, it does not mean that God will not hold you responsible for not complying with His Word. *"For if after they have escaped the pollutions of the world through the knowledge of the Lord and Saviour Jesus Christ, they are again entangled therein, and overcome, the latter end is worse with them than the beginning. For it had been better for them not to have known the way of righteousness, than, after they have known it, to turn from the holy commandment delivered unto them" (2 Pet. 2:20-21)*.

My friends, you must not get caught up in this world, for this world is passing away and you will pass away with it. If you live for this world and follow the desires of your flesh, your destination is hell. *"Love not the world, neither the things that are in the world. If any man love the world, the love of the Father is not in him" (1 John 2:15)*. Only God's children hear His voice and obey His commands. Who are you? Does God know you? Are you called according to His purpose? The time is at hand when the true worshipers of God must stand firm on God's Word. Many are called, but few are chosen. Which one are you? What are you looking for?

Chapter Eight:

The Tyrant

*T*he world has done an excellent job in creating the negative stereotype of an overbearing, loudmouth husband who disrespects and mistreats his wife. When I was a young boy, I enjoyed watching the show "The Honeymooners." The show was very entertaining. It was based on the concept of the husband working and the wife staying at home. One of the reasons for my interest was the confrontational relationship that sometimes arose between Ralph and his wife Alice. When Ralph would return home from work, he would shout, **"Alice! I'm home! Where's my dinner?"** I would just love this part when he would make his entrance. Ralph would normally continue his tirade and say, "I'm the king of my castle. I work all day long, and all I ask for is a hot dinner waiting for me when I come home." What I later learned as an adult is that this is not the best way to romance your wife. For years I found this type of humor enjoyable and relaxing. What I found out later on in life is why I enjoyed this type of authoritative humor. As a young man I perceived this show as depicting men as leaders and conquerors! I realized as I grew older how easy it was to buy in to an image of female inferiority. According to the Scriptures, this is false and outside the will of God. The Lord has placed the husband as the head of his wife. However, we are all parts of the same body. Is the heart more important than the brain? I don't think so.

Is the hand more important than the feet? I believe not. So why do we think that a man is superior to a woman? I can plainly tell you that it is purely ignorance on the part of some men. Some would ask how would you explain 1 Peter 3:7, which says that women are the weaker vessel. Jesus plainly points out that the leaders should be the servants. The greatest among men should be the servant of men. The world perceives a servant as someone who is weak. However, the Bible states that the person who is considered great among mankind is the one who is its servant. *"But it shall not be so among you: but whosoever will be great among you, let him be your minister: And whosoever will be chief among you, let him be your servant. Even as the Son of man came not to be ministered unto, but to minister, and to give his life a ransom for many"* (Matt. 20:26–28).

The first shall be last and the last first. A virtuous

The Tyrant

woman is a gift from God, and when you find such a woman, it is like finding treasure in the middle of the sea. The word "weaker" simple means "not as strong as." God has made men physically stronger than women. This does not mean inferior, but different. Men were made to work in the fields and endure hardship and pain through laborious and strenuous work. God has given man the responsibility to provide and protect his wife and family. However, America has taken this to mean that women are inferior if they remain under submission to their own husbands. The world has truly turned against God's Word. Unbelievers would rather have a lie than the truth, for a lie they will believe, but the truth they will forsake and turn away from it. *"And because I tell you the truth, ye believe me not. Which of you convinceth me of sin? And if I say the truth, why do ye not believe me? He that is of God heareth God's words: ye therefore hear them not, because ye are not of God" (John 8:45–47).*

The wife is to submit to the authority of her husband, not to mankind in general. However, this does not mean by nature that the woman is inferior to her husband. In a marriage, two people become one flesh through the joining of their souls, spirits, and bodies. To keep this unique bond from destroying itself, God has charged the man to lead and the woman to submit.

The Bible exhorts women to observe the behavior of Sarah who was obedient and submissive unto her husband. In return, Abraham was honorable and respectful unto his wife. *"For after this manner in the old time the holy women also, who trusted in God, adorned themselves, being in subjection unto their own husbands: Even as Sara obeyed Abraham, calling him lord: whose daughters ye are, as long as ye do well, and are not afraid with any amazement. Likewise, ye husbands, dwell with them according to knowledge, giving honour unto the wife, as unto the weaker vessel, and as being heirs together of the grace of life; that your prayers be not hindered"* (1 Pet. 3:5–7). The relationship between man and wife is not to be based on the premise of "if you wash my back, I'll wash yours." This is not how the Lord intended for us to interact with one another. If we are not in one accord with our spouses, are prayers will be hindered. If problems exist within the marriage, the husband is commanded to love his wife even though she may not be acting right toward him. The wife is commanded by God to do likewise. If the wife is not acting honorably, the husband is still commanded to be honorable to her. We are to treat our wives and husbands as if we were dealing with Christ. Women, this is God's truth. This is His plan. It does not matter if you do not feel comfortable submitting yourself to your husband.

God understands your plight. You married your husband and made yourself one with him before the sight of almighty God. Allow your husband to lead.

If your husband is not a Christian, the Bible states that you are to remain with him and live a life that is pleasing to God in front of your husband. Through your chaste behavior, God may use you to humble your husband. *"And unto the married I command, yet not I, but the Lord, Let not the wife depart from her husband: But and if she depart, let her remain unmarried or be reconciled to her husband: and let not the husband put away his wife. But to the rest speak I, not the Lord: If any brother hath a wife that believeth not, and she be pleased to dwell with him, let him not put her away. And the woman which hath an husband that believeth not, and if he be pleased to dwell with her, let her not leave him. For the unbelieving husband is sanctified by the wife, and the unbelieving wife is sanctified by the husband: else were your children unclean; but now are they holy. But if the unbelieving depart, let him depart. A brother or a sister is not under bondage in such cases: but God hath called us to peace. For what knowest thou, O wife, whether thou shalt save thy husband? or how knowest thou, O man, whether thou shalt save thy wife?" (1 Cor. 7:10–16).*

I realize that we live in a country that does not hold to these biblical truths. This nation will be judged for its sinful ways. However, you must remove yourself from the evil influences and corrupt doctrine that have infiltrated the world and the modern-day church. In World War II, when men were ordered to go to war, they left their homes and their wives in financial difficulty. Many women were left to work to feed their children and keep the families from being financially destitute. However, sad to say, America has led the way for many women to forsake God's ordained plan for the family. Many women love the idea of making their own money. Most men are overjoyed by the prospect of not being the sole breadwinners for their families. Consequently, this has created a problem in the culture. Many couples wonder why they do not get along. Many marriages end in divorce due to adultery and even murder. We have become a nation of hypocrites. We worship God in a fraudulent manner. The heart of America is far from God but close to His wrath. *"Ye hypocrites, well did Esaias prophesy of you, saying, This people draweth nigh unto me with their mouth, and honoureth me with their lips; but their heart is far from me. But in vain they do worship me, teaching for doctrines the commandments of men"* (Matt. 15:7–9).

The truth of the matter is that many women desire to be the heads of their households and to usurp authority over the men. This is the spirit of Eve under Satan's influence. I realize that many women would say that they have to act like men, because many men do not take on the responsibility of being men. However, this does not create an excuse for women to leave their God-given roles and pervert God's Word! If a man does not comply with the Word of God, God will judge that man. If a woman does not hold on and live according to God's Word, God will judge her, too.

Many women have been caught up in the worldly idea of "if it is good for a man, it's even better for a woman." The majority of women who attend church today would say they would like to marry Christian men. However, many churches, families, and young women are ignorant of what constitutes a true Christian man. They are ignorant of God's Word; thus they enter into unhappy, unspiritual marriages. The reason is simply this: many men and women lack home biblical training. This statement may upset some; however, I'm not writing this book to be politically correct. I'm writing to you in the name of Jesus Christ to help those who wish to be helped and to point out an evil within our society. Many of our young men and women do not have a clue about how they ought to conduct themselves. The simple reason is that no one is home raising our children. The Bible says that a woman should stay home, raise the children, and respect her husband.

Men are commanded to love and cherish their wives and to provide for their families. The majority of men and women do not adhere to this scriptural mandate given by God. Do you think that God will just put aside part of His Word, and will not hold us responsible to follow His commandments? *"I will therefore put you in remembrance, though ye once knew this, how that the Lord, having saved the people out of the land of Egypt, afterward destroyed them that believed not. And the angels which kept not their first estate, but left their own habitation, he hath reserved in everlasting chains under darkness unto the judgment of the great day. Even as Sodom and Gomorrha, and the cities about them in like manner, giving themselves over to fornication, and going after strange flesh, are set forth for an example, suffering the vengeance of eternal fire"* (Jude 5–7).

I understand that many will not agree with this book. I acknowledge that we live in a society that makes it difficult to live as Christ commanded. However, with Jesus, all things are possible. Do you believe this is true? If you truly believe God's Word, you know that the only way to be in compliance is to live according to His Word. *"And hereby we do know that we know him, if we keep his commandments. He that saith, I know him, and keepeth not his commandments, is a liar, and the truth is not in him. But whoso keepeth his word, in him verily is the love of God perfected: hereby know we that we are in him" (1 John 2:3–5).* If you love this world, you cannot comply with God's Word. This is why people have already gathered themselves preachers and teachers who will compromise God's Word. Many desire a gospel that would fit into their sinful nature. *"For the time will come when they will not endure sound doctrine; but after their own lusts shall they heap to themselves teachers, having itching ears; And they shall turn away their ears from the truth, and shall be turned unto fables" (2 Tim. 4:3–4).* The countdown has already begun. Jesus is standing on the doorstep of heaven. Are you prepared for Him to come? Are you **ready to go?**

Chapter Nine:

The Unbreakable
Do You Take This Woman To Be Your Wife?

*I*f you are married, you have heard these words before: "Do you take this person to be your lawfully wedded wife or husband?" This is normally the moment when people start to cry in the congregation. The minister is now inquiring about the commitment of the two participants.

This is the moment when the bride and the groom will seal their marriage contract in front of family, friends, and, most importantly, the almighty God! The minister finally asks the question to the groom: "Do you take this woman to be your lawfully wedded wife, to love and to cherish, for richer or poorer, in sickness and in health, till **death** do you part?" If you are married, you have already said *I do!* My brothers and sisters, your own words may have put you in jeopardy of hell. *"And I say unto you, Whosoever shall put away his wife, except it be for fornication, and shall marry another, committeth adultery: and whoso marrieth her which is put away doth commit adultery" (Matt. 19:9). "The wife is bound by the law as long as her husband liveth; but if her husband be dead, she is at liberty to be married to whom she will; only in the Lord" (1 Cor. 7:39).* However, I realize that many people were married and divorced before knowing God's Word and have since remarried. If you are in this situation, in the name of the Lord, cry out to Him for mercy. Repent to God for your earlier decision, stay married, and love your mate as the Bible says (1 Cor. 7:24).

This biblical mandate may offend some of you. However, who would we rather please, men or God? For me, that's not even a question. For while I'm alive, I will live for Jesus, and when I die, I will gain eternal life with Him. *"For to me to live is Christ, and to die is gain" (Phil. 1:21).* Therefore, I must teach and preach God's Word. I realize that many of you may be disgruntled or perhaps angry. However, your anger is a testimony against you, for all of God's children will obey His Word, and His Word will not be grievous. *"By this we know that we love the children of God, when we love God, and keep his commandments. For this is the love of God, that we keep his commandments: and his com-*

mandments are not grievous" (1 John 5:2–3). God's Word is the judgment upon the world, and I am a willing prisoner of the Lord, proclaiming what has already been written.

If you are living under this situation, instead of getting upset with me, search the Scriptures and work out your own salvation. Jesus said that only His sheep hear His voice. Can you hear Jesus? I hope so. The Word of God has stipulated that the husband should dwell with his wife according to knowledge, and give her honor as his wife. These two requirements that God has placed at the feet of men are essential, if we as men are going to live as the Scriptures have commanded. When we honor our wives, we honor ourselves and, more importantly, the Lord Jesus Christ. For what Christian who loves the Lord would live a life of dishonesty before his spouse? When a husband and wife obey these mandates from God, their relationship is one of honesty and integrity. When this occurs, they will be fulfilling what God had commissioned them to do: to dwell with honor with each other, and conform to the Word of God. ***This is the Christian marriage!***

As we have found out from reading this book, the Word of God is being blasphemed when men and women leave their God-given roles and responsibilities and cleave to the doctrine of demons. The book of Jude describes a period of time when the Word of God will be blasphemed and compromised. Many people will be confused and disillusioned from what is the true Word of God. However, you have now been enlightened to the plan that God has set forth for the true Christian family. *"And hereby we do know that we know him, if we keep his commandments. He that saith, I know him, and keepeth not his commandments, is a liar, and the truth is not in him. But whoso keepeth his word, in him verily is the love of God perfected: hereby know we that we are in him" (1 John 2:3–5).* When we keep God's commandments, we will know that we are true Christians. If a man says he knows God and does not keep His commandments, he is a liar, and the truth is not in him.

The first step to being free from this sin of disobedience is to repent to God for your wayward and ignorant practice. Most people have been ignorant of the fact that God never intended for women to work outside of the home. For when the woman leaves the home, the family is neglected due to her lack of guidance, care, and supervision. God wishes to bless the family. However, families are left without God's blessing because they are living under a curse.

I understand that many couples may read this book and say that they are financially in debt and unable to comply with this mandate from God. Others will state that God understands their situation and will excuse them for not being in compliance with His Word. **(Don't believe that lie!)** My friends, the time is at hand when the true worshipers of God will worship him in spirit and in truth. *"But the hour cometh, and now is, when the true worshippers shall worship the Father in spirit and in truth: for the Father seeketh such to worship him. God is a Spirit: and they that worship him must worship*

The Unbreakable

him in spirit and in truth" (John 4:23–24). You cannot explain away this God-given commandment for the woman to remain at home and raise her children. God has commanded for women to submit themselves to their husbands. The husband is mandated by God to love his wife and provide for the family. We cannot run from the truth. The truth will find us out. If we love the world, we will sell out our wives, daughters, and, most importantly, almighty God.

The reason why I can say this is because the world is inside of the modern-day church (the whore). The true church is scattered throughout the world, waiting for the Savior Jesus Christ to return and gather us unto Himself. We have reached a point in the history of mankind where the church is driving solo. For Jesus is on the outside of the church knocking to the inhabitants inside. *"As many as I love, I rebuke and chasten: be zealous therefore, and repent. Behold, I stand at the door, and knock: if any man hear my voice, and open the door, I will come in to him, and will sup with him, and he with me. To him that overcometh will I grant to sit with me in my throne, even as I also overcame, and am set down with my Father in his throne" (Rev. 3:19–21).*

This is a sad time for many people who are trying to find out the truth of God's Word. The Bible tells us that a time will come when men and women must have the Word of God hidden in their hearts. For the time will come when we will search for the truth and will not be able to find it. The world has deceived and hindered the true message of Jesus Christ. Some may have read this book and want to be set free, no longer wanting to be on the wrong side of God's will and plan for the family. We must stop training our daughters to be like men. We must encourage our wives to trust in us and forsake the temptations of the auction block. Brothers and sisters, it's time to remove our families out of the mouth of the wolf. It's time for us to maintain the unbreakable bond and to set the captives free. Escort your wife off the auction block. It's time to be set free from the bondage of the curse that God bestowed upon man from the beginning of time. For the curse has infected this generation of the cover-girl magazine era. Today's women desire to be noticed and wanted. They accent certain parts of their bodies to gain attention from others. But their souls resemble a prostitute selling her body for a ten-dollar quickie. Many of today's women have sold their bodies and their souls for an annual salary at the J.O.B.

It's time to let Jesus in! He can escort you off your spiritual street corner. You no longer have to sell yourself at the work place. Jesus can set you free from this life of spiritual prostitution. It's time for men to stop acting like pimps and start acting like husbands. **We must support our wives spiritually and financially!** The time is now at hand, and the trumpet is preparing to blow. Jesus is coming back, and He's looking for His bride. He went away to prepare a place for us. However, while Jesus was gone, the whore who falsely calls herself the bride of Christ has practiced adultery against Him. This prostitute has slept with the world and the perverse doctrines of demons. Those who claimed to love Jesus have been shacking up with Satan. Many have sold out the Master for a J.O.B. Many have sold their souls to the father of liars for the riches of this world. Woman, you must ask yourself this question: have you sold your soul to the devil for a nine-to-five job or for a cushy corner office with some fancy tittle? If so, this makes you no better than a spiritual prostitute, for you have jeopardized the unbreakable bond.

Many couples have fallen in love with the so-called American dream. Consequently, they have abandoned the Word of God at the expense of their children. However, the world is fading away and Satan, who is your true lover, will forsake you because he does not love you. Satan looks at you as a quick and easy conquest. He loathes you and wishes to see you in hell. My friends, our lives are like a vapor—we are here today and gone tomorrow. Your life is a story that is being told for the whole world and heaven to see. Who are you? Are you still a prostitute who would sell yourself for an annual salary? Or are you that born-again woman in Christ ready to stand on the **Word of God?** I truly understand that many women desire to be in compliance with the Word of God.

However, for many single mothers who have no other means of providing for the family, or for the wife whose husband is unable or unwilling to work, God understands your plight, for you are being made to work like a man because you have no husband to provide. In these cases, the church should help provide and take care of you. In this day and age, that is not going to happen. My sisters, God will not hold you responsible in these cases.

Earlier in this book, I pointed out a few examples of sinful deeds that one person could perpetrate against another. When you are forced to do something against your will, God does not hold you responsible for that action. For an example, the crime rate pertaining to rape and child molestation is at an all-time high, sad to say. When one of these offenses are committed, the perpetrator of the crime is punished and the victim is consoled. When Amnon raped his sister Tamar, he took away her virginity and her innocence. Would we say that Tamar committed fornication and incest with her brother? Or would we say that Amnon committed the fornication and incest against her? Amnon was the one punished for this evil deed, not Tamar. A child is not held responsible for the sexual molestation that is done against him, for a child is under the authority of his parents. The wife is in a similar situation, for God has placed her under the authority of her husband. If the husband takes advantage of his wife and makes her work against her will, the husband is held accountable. Nevertheless, the wife is being defiled when she is made to work outside of the home in the same way Amnon defiled Tamar when he raped her. Under these situations, God does not hold the victim responsible, only the perpetrator. However, for those women who are married and have children who are working because they want to fulfill their own ambitions, God will repay. Many claim to love Jesus, and yet they do not adhere to the vows that they proclaimed when they supposedly

The Unbreakable

became believers.

Many couples will conspire to defy God in tandem. I classify such a couple as the tag-team duo. This is when the husband and the wife are in full agreement with her working outside of the home under the authority of someone else. Marriages are defiled and families are perverted when the wife is working outside of the home.

My friends, we most have the faith and commitment of Hosea. Hosea was an Old Testament prophet who God ordained to marry a prostitute. His wife, Gomer, was unfaithful to him. She was a beautiful woman. Her gift of satanic seduction was mesmerizing to men. She embraced man after man into her bosom. She defiled her marriage and dishonored her husband. Yet Hosea still took her back. However, it did not matter, for she would go right back into her lovers' arms. It was only when her lovers had forsaken her and sold her into slavery that she was humbled. By this time, her beauty had faded and her satanic seduction was gone. Satan had used her up, or so he thought. As she was being paraded around the auction block, she noticed a man who looked familiar—it was Hosea. Hosea paid the price to take her off the auction block. As Hosea was taking her away, she thanked him by calling him Master. Hosea, after hearing how Gomer addressed him by calling him Master, responded with love in his eyes, and said to Gomer, "I'm not your master, I'm your husband. Come down from the auction block."

Come, all who are on the Lord's side. For Jesus Christ is standing on the doorstep of heaven waiting to bring His bride home to His Father. But will He find faith on the earth when He comes? My friends, hearken to the words of the Lord, for He is worthy to be praised. Let heaven and earth remain silent, for His Word created the heavens and the earth. The rocks will cry out "hallelujah" as they recognize Him as the King of Kings and the Lord of Lords. Let man stand still and observe the salvation of the Lord. For we have been bought with a price.

Chapter Ten:

No Weapon Formed Against Us Shall Prosper!

For all practical purposes, the modern-day church is not the true church. The church age is over. God has removed His Holy Spirit from the corporate church, but not from His elect. Satan now sits in the temple (in the people) impersonating the bride of Christ, but in reality is a prostitute. About two thousand years ago, the disciples of Jesus Christ began building on the foundation of the church. Jesus laid the groundwork and the foundation. As we stand here today, God has already reserved for Himself His elect from out of the church. God has placed a burden in the hearts of His elect to cry out to the world, and particularly to the inhabitants who remain in worship with the whore. My fellow brothers and sisters, who have been saved by the grace of our Lord and Savior Jesus Christ, fear not the devil. God has called you for His divine purpose. No weapon formed against us shall prosper (Isa. 54:17).

As we turn the tables of time and look back on the history of Israel, we will notice a distinct time in her history when she was under Babylonian rule. Israel was a rebellious people who lacked faith in the unshakable Word of God. When Israel was free from the tyranny of slavery, she rebelled against the law of God. Therefore, God used Babylon to chastise Israel. The rulers of Babylon presented a constant and ever-present reminder to the Israelites that they were in captivity. The Babylonians were unbelievers in the Word of God and lived under a system that practiced and promoted idol worship. God allowed Israel to remain in bondage because of her disobedience to Him. However, during this time of enslavement, Israel remained faithful.

Nevertheless, God knew the nature of Israel, for He knew that when times were good, the Israelites would forsake Him and worship the gods of Satan. God gave the Israelites prophets and they killed them; He gave them the commandments and they ignored them. He gave them the Pentateuch, which is the law, and they broke the law. Even after all this, God delivered them out of bondage by first allowing them to go through a tribulation, which was their captivity under Babylonian rule. Israel had a covenant with God; and He always keeps His promise.

No Weapon Formed Against Us Shall Prosper!

God ordained from the foundation of the world this present time that we live in. He has adopted us into the royal family, making us fellow heirs of the royal priesthood. Since this adoption contract was fulfilled before the foundation of the world, it's time for us to understand our inheritance. Ephesians 1:3–6 states that the Gentiles should be fellow heirs and of the same body and partakers of God's promise in Christ Jesus. Therefore, if we are fellow heirs with Christ, we have what Jesus has. All glory is His, all praise is His, all joy is His, and all salvation is His. His joy is our joy, His victory is our victory, and His peace is our peace, for we are joint heirs with Christ. We shall reign and rule with him—this is our inheritance. However, if we live for Christ Jesus, we shall be persecuted for righteousness' sake. My friends, know and understand this: Jesus came and preached to His own people, the Israelites, and His own rejected him. You will face trials and tribulations in this world if you live for Jesus. For His pain is our pain, His sorrow is our sorrow, and His tears are our tears, for it is no longer we who live, but Christ who lives within us. Behold, the old things have passed away, and all things have become new. His battle is our battle. As Moses stood before the Israelites, I stand before you today. All who are on the Lord's side, let them come! Oh, hear the voice of the Lord, for He is calling us by our first names. He is standing at the gates of heaven, waiting to take us home. Oh, can you hear the voice of the Lord?

He came for those who are sick, not for those who are

well. He came for those who realize that they are naked and have lost their way. He came for the weak, not for the strong. He came for the sinner, not the righteous. Oh, my friends, without Jesus we are naked and destitute; we're lost in the valley of despair. We have no strength or power to heal ourselves; we are in bondage to the ailments of sin. But Jesus is the Balm of Gilead.

We must humble ourselves so that God can elevate us. We must not think highly of ourselves lest we fall. Those who are called by His Sprit shall live by His Spirit. For the fruit of the Spirit is love, joy, peace, longsuffering, gentleness, goodness, faith, meekness, and temperance; against such things there is no law. If you are in Jesus Christ, you have crucified the flesh with the affections to do lustful things. If we live in the Spirit, let us also walk in the Spirit. Let us not desire vainglory, provoking one another and envying one another. We ought to bear one another's burdens. If a man believes himself to be holy and is nothing, he fools himself.

Listen and learn the will of the devil. Satan wishes to sift you like wheat; he wants to destroy you, for you have inherited the kingdom of God. You have entered into the knowledge of truth. For you have judged those who came to you in sheep's clothing and have recognized them as wolves. You are now on the hit list of Satan because you have exposed his identity and have rebuked him before the world. Therefore, he will seek to destroy you. But as God said to Isaiah, I say to you that no weapon formed against you shall prosper! God will make your enemies your footstool, for He said to our enemies to not touch His anointed and do His servants no harm. Stand firm on God's Word; don't let the enemy overtake you. For God has called you out of darkness into His marvelous light. Be strong in the Lord and in the power of His might. Pray that God will use you for His glory. God says that all glory, peace, deliverance, hope, dominion, joy, and power are His. Your house and all that you have are His. God is omnipotent, omniscient, and omnipresent. No weapon formed against us shall ever prosper.

They may try to curse your name, but their tongues will be quieted; they may try to dig a ditch for you, but that ditch is not for you. God will ensnare them in their own wickedness and bury them in their sins. God has set you apart for His service and for His will. Think not that Jesus came to bring peace on the earth—He came to bring a sword. He came to bring division between a son and his father, a daughter and her mother, and a husband and his wife.

Do you understand what I'm saying to you today? You cannot compromise God's Word just because it does not fit well into your lifestyle or your mindset. If you love your family more than you love Jesus, you are not worthy to be called a child of God and you have been found ineligible to inherit His kingdom.

Oh, how I love Jesus, for He is my anchor in the time of the storm. He will protect us from our enemies and deliver us from our adversaries. A crown is waiting for each of us on the other side of glory. Hear the voice of the Lord, for He has declared that He has chosen us. We have been bought with a price; and Jesus paid that price. He purchased us on the cross, when He shed His blood for the remission of our sins. We were dead in our sins and He made us alive. Therefore, we have dominion over sin and have been saved by grace, for no weapon formed against shall prosper!

Chapter Eleven:

Yesterday

*A*s I conclude this book, I pray for your spiritual growth and understanding of the Word of God.

I desire that God's Spirit would dwell with you, as a flower prepares to bloom for spring and as the rain falls from the sky to beautify the green grass of the field. I pray that God will bring you out of fellowship with the great whore. If we remain in fellowship with the prostitute in the pulpit, we are placing ourselves in the line of fire. We are sleeping with the enemy. We have a name but no cause, a house but no home, a song without a melody, and a message without the Word! As the sun rises in the east and sets in the west, the Lord will hold us accountable for what we do. We must put away foolish things and hold firm to the unchangeable Word of

God. We must die to our flesh and cry out to God for mercy, for the flesh is nothing but ashes and dust.

The Lord has troubled my spirit concerning you. The reason why a preacher preaches is because the Spirit of God moves upon him and creates a godly concern for the children of God. The world is fading away; the return of Jesus is soon to come, and the prostitute is in the pulpit. Wake up, my brothers and sisters, and come out from among her and be not partakers of her sin. For the prostitute in the pulpit has created her own righteousness and her own gospel. She has corrupted untold billions of people, for she is the wife of Satan and is submissive to his will.

Satan has called to himself false ministers of light to excite and pacify the members of this false church for the purpose of capturing their souls. God does not hear the prayers of this whore, for she speaks with the blood of the saints on her hands. May God empower your family and direct you in all that you do. Hold firm to the Word of God, for no weapon formed against you shall prosper. As I close this last chapter in this book, I pray that it will not be the last chapter in your life. Lord willing, it is the Lord's plan that you will be saved. I pray that you cry out to God for mercy on your soul so that you will not stand with the prostitute in the pulpit on the last day!

Before we close, I want you to know who I am. I am the son of Frank and Barbara Copeland, the father of Breanna and Candace Copeland, and the husband of one wife, Yvonne Copeland. However, far more important

Yesterday

than these, I am a child of God. The blood of the Lamb has redeemed me. For I am a sinner saved by grace. I am not worthy to even mention the name of the Lord, but he had mercy on me. Jesus is Lord! Who else is worthy to stand before the throne of God, and what man would dare deny His Word? I would like to thank my wife and children for their support over the years as I wrestled with this book and the trials and tribulations it has brought my way. I would also like to acknowledge my grandmothers, Lillian and Ella-Mae, who have crossed the river of time to hopefully go home with Jesus.

My friends, this life is only for a moment. We all will have to stand before God on Judgment Day, when we will be confronted with yesterday. I believe we all have known someone who has crossed the river of time. We all have experienced the joy of thinking about the past. We can remember when we were children and the exhilaration of playing with our friends and the joy of laughter. Life seemed so effortless and free of responsibilities and the consequences of sin. When we were children, most of us depended on our parents for our survival.

However, as we grow older and go through the timetable of life and enter into adulthood, we find ourselves on a continual journey through the oracles of time, trying to find our way. As we experience life, we deal with the many surprises it may have to offer. As mature adults, we find ourselves burdened down with the responsibilities of paying bills, raising children, paying mortgages, and growing old. Many people look back on their lives wonder where it all went. They begin to question the purpose of life. As we grow older and begin to feel the effects of age, such as arthritis in our bones or a little balding or gray in our hair, we start to experience the breakdown of our bodies and the humanity of our being. We may start to think back on yesterday. We will start to remember how it used to be and what we used to able to do. We may even gather the children around and inform them that we were not always like this, that we too used to be young and vibrant and in good physical health. However, as we stand here in the reality of our own mortality, I'm reminded of these words: *"I have been young, and now am old; yet have I not seen the righteous forsaken, nor his seed begging bread" (Ps. 37:25). "Verily, verily, I say unto thee, When thou wast young, thou girdedst thyself, and walkedst whither thou wouldest: but when thou shalt be old, thou shalt stretch forth thy hands, and another shall gird thee, and carry thee whither thou wouldest not" (John 21:18).*

As I have mentioned earlier in this book, the world we live in places special emphasis on our outward appearance. Most of us have heard the often-quoted Scripture that man looks at the outside, but God looks at the inside. Even though many of us have read this Scripture, very few of us concern ourselves with the essence of its meaning. The Bible clearly states that God does not dwell in a building made by the hands of man, but He dwells in the body of the believer, His elect. It is the body, the temple of God, in which the Holy Spirit dwells. *"Know ye not that ye are the temple of God, and that the Spirit of God dwelleth in you? If any man defile the temple of God, him shall God destroy; for the temple of God is holy, which temple ye are" (1 Cor. 3:16–17).*

My friends, if we belong to or visit a church, we are grieving the Spirit of God that dwells in us. The building could be filled to capacity, the choir could be singing, the trumpets could be blowing, and the organist could be playing—it does not matter, for the Holy Spirit no longer acknowledges the corporate church. God does not dwell in the pews, the choir loft, or the pulpit. He dwells in the body of the elect. It is an indictment on so-called believers when the lives we proclaim are in stark contrast to the lives we live. The Bible says that where two or more are gathered in His name, there He is in the midst of them. But God does not dwell in disobedience. Come out from among that whore! If the corporate church building is filled to capacity, it does not matter, for the assembly is void of God's presence. God is not there. Your worship is in vain! God no longer recognizes this form of worship, for Satan has taken it over. A building cannot preach the gospel, nor can it praise God. Many people today are living their lives as if it were yesterday. They are holding on to the old form of worship, which is the old synagogue worship, where people put all their resources and time into a building. My friends, we have been witnesses and we can attest that the world is living according to its own desires and has trampled on the sanctified Word of God.

Many who claim to be holy and true have turned their hearts away from the truth. They are searching for yesterday. They are embracing a different gospel that appeals to their lifestyles and the desires of their hearts. They may desire to shout hallelujah, but their praise is in vain, for they lack the truth in their hearts to shout truthfully. They want yesterday, but yesterday is gone, never to rise again. Yesterday's promise is tomorrow's memory. Many have lost their way and have forsaken the hope of salvation. Jesus is the hope of His people. Jesus can make a way out of no way. He turned water into wine, gave sight to the blind, hope for the hopeless, peace in the time of the storm, and salvation to those He has called. Many people, sad to say, use yesterday to relive lost expectations. Yesterday, for many people hold lost dreams and dashed hopes. Yesterday represents missed opportunities and failed relationships.

We have entered into perilous times when men and women love themselves more than then they love God. The unsaved world has turned to Satan and holds to the practices of demons. Many yearn for yesterday, for they know that tomorrow is judgment. Some may feel enslaved to the sins of yesterday. We may feel bound and that Satan has defeated us. We may find ourselves crying out for help, but help seems so far away. I will tell you the same thing my grandmother told me when she was alive. She would say, "Mark, search the Scriptures, where you will find your hope for salvation." Satan understands that within the Scriptures is the solution for yesterday.

Time is running out, and God will set all things in order when He comes. We have been desensitized to sin. The whole world is in the hands of the evil one. Men and

Yesterday

women are in bondage to their flesh and are held in spiritual captivity. The spirit of perversion has been let loose on this last generation. Can you see what I can see? Men and women are being attacked by the demon of homosexuality. Men are fathering babies and leaving mothers to fend for themselves. Young girls are being led unto unspeakable lusts. Consequently, many young girls find themselves pregnant and tragically turning to abortion, believing they have found the solution to their problem. We live in a time where husbands devalue their wives and dishonor their vows.

Hear and understand what I am saying. We have all sinned and come short of the glory of God. This is why He came out of heaven took on an earthly body and called Himself Jesus. He provided Himself for our redemption so that we no longer are bound to practice sin. The true tragedy of sin is not sin itself, but remaining in sin once you have been set free. If we denounce the Bible as old-fashioned and out of touch with society, how will we escape from the torment of sin? God wants to set us free from the captivity of sin. God desires to deliver His elect from the demons of fornication, adultery, homosexuality, and the lusts of the flesh. We may desire to be free from our past mistakes, the devaluing of our bodies, and the perversion of our minds. We want our yesterdays to be gone and thrown into the sea of forgetfulness and to never be raised again. However, sad to say, we continue to live lives of rebellion toward God. We are products of our society, the offspring of the mother of harlots. We have been set up to live lives of

The Prostitute in the Pulpit

rebellion toward God.

Oh, America, the nation that perverts its youth, effeminizes its women, and emasculates its men, God will surly remember your sins. You have sold yourself to the highest bidder and have spiritually fornicated with the world for the pleasures of this world. You have entered into buildings and sanctuaries and have impersonated the true bride of Christ. You have defiled yourself for silver and gold, and have gathered yourselves spiritual prostitutes impersonating pastors to seduce your soul.

Who will stand against Satan and his army? Heaven and earth will pass away, but God's Word will never pass away. Jesus is the Word. If we deny the Bible, we deny Jesus. The Lord desires to create in us a holy and acceptable sacrifice. He wishes to purify us with His Word. God wants to fill us with His power. Once we receive His power, we will be able to walk through the valley of the shadow of death and fear no evil. We will be able to walk and not be weary, to run and not faint. Yesterday is gone and tomorrow is yet to come. But today is the day of our salvation. Stand tall and hold firm to your faith. Don't waver nor bow to the attacks of the enemy. Yesterday is gone and tomorrow is yet to come, but today is the day of salvation. Come out from the prostitute in the pulpit and be ye separate, saith the Lord!

Yesterday

April 23, 2002

Brother Harold Camping
Family Radio
290 Hegenberger Road
Oakland, CA 94621

Dear Brother Camping:

I bring you greetings in the name of our Lord and Savior Jesus Christ. I realize that your time is valuable, so I will be brief.

I thank the Lord for you and family radio. Your ministry has been a blessing and an inspiration to me to stand on the infallible Word of God. In January 1996, I began writing a book concerning the false church and the downfall of the family. The Lord placed a burden in my heart to preach and teach this message to anyone who would listen.

As I began my journey, I found it to be a lonely one. My pastor and other church leaders rejected me concerning the message that the Holy Spirit is no longer in the corporate church. I should not have been surprised by their hostility, but I was. It saddened me to see their anger toward me. Consequently, I took my family out of the church and began home Bible fellowship. During this time, I put the book project on hold due to my own insecurities and failure to stand strong for the Lord in the face of persecution.

However, in December of 2001 as I was traveling from North Carolina to New Jersey, I turned my radio to Open Forum. I had not heard the program since April of 2000, which is when I moved from New Jersey to North Carolina. During that Open Forum program is when I first learned that the Lord had given you the same message that he had given me. Praise the Lord for your faithfulness, even though evil is spoken against you and Family Radio for your God-inspired message. Because of your faithfulness, the Lord has used you and Family Radio to help inspire me to finish writing my book. Your ministry has been a tremendous blessing to my family and me. I would like to see it continue to prosper and grow so that it can continue to reach throughout the world the elect of God.

Your brother in Christ,

Mark E. Copeland